PRAISE FOR MARY KATHERINE BACKSTROM

"One of Facebook's funniest parents!"
—TODAY Parenting Team, the *TODAY Show*

*"Mary Katherine brings love, wisdom, compassion, humor,
and insight to her writing that is a must read for every parent."*
—Love What Matters

*"I love how honest and relatable Mary Katherine is in her writing. When an author is
raw, it is easy to make a connection to their work."*
—Meredith Masony, Founder of That's Inappropriate

"Thank you for cracking us up."
—*TODAY* with Hoda & Jenna

*"I have probably read more parenting essays than anyone on the planet,
and Mary Katherine's voice still surprises me. I laugh out loud, cry, and
recall the magic of being a mother in those fresh early years. She is a
friend to the struggling moms in the trenches of motherhood."*
– Jill Smokler, founder of Scary Mommy and *New York Times* best-selling author

THE MESSY TRUTH ABOUT MOTHERHOOD

Mom Babble

MARY KATHERINE BACKSTROM

Abingdon Press™

Growing in Life, Serving in Faith

MOM BABBLE

THE MESSY TRUTH ABOUT MOTHERHOOD

ISBN 978-1-5018-9452-7

19 20 21 22 23 24 25 26 27 28—10 9 8 7 6 5 4 3 2 1

MANUFACTURED IN THE PEOPLE'S REPUBLIC OF CHINA

TO MAMA, WHO SURVIVED MY FERAL CHILDHOOD AND
TAUGHT ME EVERY GOOD THING ABOUT MOTHERHOOD . . .
AND TO IAN, WHO LOVES ME WITH MORE GRACE
THAN I'LL EVER DESERVE.

CONTENTS

FOREWORD

FROM MEREDITH MASONY — FOUNDER OF THAT'S INAPPROPRIATE

Life is funny. I met Mary Katherine a few years back at a blogging conference. She was the short lady screaming "y'all" in the hotel hallway, inviting everyone up to her room.

Mary Katherine is a kind, loving soul, who loves God and her family. When she gets off her fanny and writes, it's simply amazing. Mary Katherine likes to hug. Like a lot. In contrast to her personality, I am a rather blunt person, who isn't much for hugs. Picture a cactus, and now put my head on it. We are an odd pair to say the least, but it makes for a great friendship. She is now known as MK to me.

While at this blogging conference, MK talked about this book she was going to write. She was all tied up in knots about it. She wasn't sure if it was the right thing to do, if she had it in her. She wasn't even sure who she was at that time. I know that as a wife, mom, and woman, I have been lost and unsure. I have been Mary Katherine. I listened as she told me about her dreams and goals. I listened as she talked about her past, her present, and what she truly wanted for her future. She asked me for some advice on writing the book, and my response was simple, "Just do it. Write the book." I continued by saying that it seemed simple, but I knew how hard that was to do. I know how messy life with kids can be. I know how many things happen in a day and by the end of it you just want to crawl in a hole and pretend you don't exist, so you can quietly eat six-month-old Halloween candy you have stolen from your kids in peace. I totally get it. But MK needed to start. She needed a kick. Let's be honest, we all need kicks.

I'm not sure how many phone conversations I've had with MK about this book, but I am so happy to say, this book is finally finished, and you are going to absolutely love it. It was "a labor of love" and you will be #Blessed to enjoy this thing . . . I promise. MK put on her big girl panties and did an amazing job, by simply starting. She started to share. She started to listen to herself, to believe in herself, and it is amazing. I am honored to call her "friend," and I am so excited for what this book means to her and for what it will mean to you.

Motherhood is extremely isolating. There are times when the journey feels like a desert island, but not the kind with beach chairs and daiquiris. The kind where *Lord of the Flies* took place. It is so important to talk about all of the aspects of motherhood, and MK did an amazing job sharing her heart and her words, so that moms can know they are not alone.

I watched MK live out a very private experience this year in a very public way. Mary Katherine had a double mastectomy, and like the brave warrior she is, she shared it with the world to help others. She is truly a woman who wants to see other women succeed and does so with grace.

MK is funny, talented, outspoken, and honest. She is a mother on a mission, and I am so proud of her. I know that as you read her words, you will be able to relate to her and take comfort in knowing you are not alone. Most of our phone calls end abruptly because one of our kids needs something or has broken something, but I always know I can call her back and she will be there.

The moral of the story is that motherhood is messy, and anytime we can find real moms who share the raw, honest, messy, and loving side of motherhood, we are winning. I do my best to deliver that message on my platform, and I am so happy Mary Katherine does it on hers. We can break down the stereotype that motherhood includes perfection and moms never yell or get it all done all of the time. The reality is so far from that expectation, and moms would feel so much better if they would stop attempting to attain unrealistic goals of motherhood.

Thank you, MK, for writing your truth. Thank you for sharing this with us, for showing the world your scars, and for letting your brave shine through.

INTRODUCTION

I have a friend who, every time I ask her to go running with me, laughs in my face.

"If you see me running, MK, you better watch out. That probably means a bear is chasing me."

Now, I am not sure if you are aware of this, but it turns out that bears are really fast. Like, thirty miles per hour fast. Which is exactly what I told my friend who hates running.

You see, as her friend, I felt obligated to let her know that should she ever encounter a bear, the best way to respond would be to accept her fate, turn around, and face the dang bear.

To which she responded, "You are so weird. Nobody hates running that much, and besides, who the heck chooses the bear?"

Confession time.

Six years ago, if an Alaskan grizzly had walked up to me all growling and mean and said, "MK, you have two choices: become a full-time mom blogger or become my next dinner," I probably would have chosen the bear.

Before my babies were born, I believed nothing could be as boring or blasé as the whole messy-bun culture of modern motherhood. I believed motherhood took normal human beings, chewed them up, and spit them out with sloppy hair and yoga pants. Mark my words, that was never going to be me.

Never. (Ever.)

When I became pregnant with my Benjamin, I had a lot of ideas about what motherhood would look like. Basically, it would look exactly like what I was already doing, but with an adorable bonus human tagging along in a stroller.

I was going to be a career woman. I was gonna stay involved in local politics. I was gonna lead worship at church, get back in shape, and stay on top of all my favorite hobbies.

There would be none of this minivan driving, mom blogging mess. I had bigger plans.

Then my son was born, and my plans went splat like a bug on a windshield.

A windshield known as postpartum depression.

That seamless transition I had planned from a childfree life to the same exact life, plus a child, just didn't happen. Motherhood humbled me. In a way, it pretty much chewed me up and spit me back out.

The best way to describe my first week at home with my son is to say I felt like I was on some trippy, out-of-control, merry-go-round. My son was the only fixed point, and everything and everyone simply revolved around him. My life, it seemed, had a new axis.

If any guests came to my house, they fussed over the baby. Cards and presents arrived by the dozen, every single one was addressed for the baby.

And while everyone buzzed over this incredible miracle that had just entered our lives, I shuffled around the house like *The Walking Dead*, feeling like an alien trapped inside a deflated balloon body.

How was I ever going to become some well-traveled, captivating career mom with interesting hobbies and a Gap model baby? I could barely complete a grocery store run without having a meltdown.

The truth is, I felt lost.

I desperately wanted to feel seen, understood, and loved. And hard as they tried, my friends without children just couldn't relate to the struggles of a woman who had sleep deprivation and bleeding nipples. (That's really just something you have to experience to understand.)

What I needed, more than anything in the world, was community.

One night, in a true fit of desperation, I sent out a parenting SOS via

Facebook. Something about teething, or sleeping, or who knows. I don't even remember. Something about mom life.

And the next thing I knew, my post was overwhelmed with support.

Messages of "I've been there" and "I'm still there" and "Don't worry, honey, this will get better."

Messages from people I hadn't talked to in twenty years. Messages from cousins I didn't know existed. I even got a message from the wife of a high school ex-boyfriend.

I mean . . . *what?*

This whole phenomenon felt . . . odd. But every single woman who reached out, no matter how different we were, offered support and solidarity.

For the first time in a month I felt heard, seen, and loved. I had to face the very real possibility that maybe those crazy messy-bun wearing women who joked about yoga pants and minivans weren't so bad after all.

That maybe . . . juuust maybe . . .

Now, I don't know if you've ever driven a Jeep before, but it's a pretty cool experience. Jeep drivers are a lovely bunch. Whenever they spot another Jeep out in traffic, they make a point to wave or honk or smile at each other. It's like they share some sort of Jeepy secret between them.

I freaking love it.

But it's nothing compared to the nod of solidarity you receive from another mom when your toddlers are melting down in an airport baggage claim at midnight. Or the "you've got this" look that passes between two parents on the first day of school, when both of their preschoolers are crying in the parking lot.

My hope for this book is that it can serve as a collection of winks and nods, from one mother to another. That my honest, messy stories of motherhood might encourage your spirit, the same way so many of you have inspired and encouraged mine over the years. I hope that when you hear my voice in these stories, you hear the voice of a friend who is waving at you from within the pages. A Jeepy little, "I see you, friend. You are not alone. We are doing this thing together with the top down, the wind in our hair, and an 80 percent chance of afternoon showers."

Oh, Mamas.

I want to thank you so much for being my people, even when I didn't think you could be. I'm sorry I judged your messy buns. Yoga pants really are the greatest. Thank you for being here for me, long before I was able to return the favor.

I love you more than words can express. Thank you, thank you for grabbing this book. I hope it touches your heart.

I hope it makes you glad I didn't choose the bear.

Love,

MK

Birth
OF A

Mother

BIRTH OF A MOTHER

SEPTEMBER 30, 2013, IS A DAY I WON'T SOON FORGET.

My life was altered completely the day I became a mother, and I'm not just talking about my sleep schedule . . . more like the entire planet shifted on its axis.

Oh yes! It's the birth story! Isn't that what people love to know? The gory, nasty, poopy details of how my baby made his way into the world?

No, you say?

That's fine. I'll skip the explicit details.

On that fateful day, I was awakened by the fragrance of raw sewage wafting through my house. I tried flushing the toilet, which responded by actually BURPING at me. The burp was followed by multiple gurgles, and pretty soon the scent of Septic Belch was fumigating the entire house. I freaked and call my landlord. No quick fix.

And with that as a backdrop for this glorious day, my uterus awoke with a yawn and said, "WOOHOO, let's have a baby, y'all!"

With good reason to escape the house, my family and I went out on a ravenous food-binge for the ages. By nine o'clock I had consumed a breakfast wrap, a pancake, two scrambled eggs and some sausage. Then we waited a couple hours and went out for Mexican.

(Stop judging me.)

Roughly 5,000 calories later, we headed to a kids' consignment shop in search of Halloween costumes. Perusing racks of doggies, princesses, hot dogs, and the like, I began to experience what mommies refer to as "contractions."

---

con·trac·tion (kən-ˈtrak shən). n.

1. The act of contracting or the state of being contracted.

2. What happens when the hand of God reaches into your uterus and gives it a tight squeeze. Over and over again.

So . . . you know that scene in Indiana Jones where the dude reaches into somebody's chest and pulls out his heart? Contractions are just like that, except your innards stay put. I reached for a cute little pumpkin costume and BAM.

I was bent over, heaving and contemplating the fact that our pancake/egg wrap/Mexican fiesta was a bad idea. Then my mom suggested that maybe it was not gas. And perhaps we should time them?

Two minutes apart—Yippee ki yay, let's go!

I showered at a friend's place and retrieved my bag from the House of Stink.

Ladies, don't lie. We've all dreamed of the "Baby is Coming!" car ride at some point. Envisioned the Hollywood version of heavy breathing, the speeding car, the frantic husband. As we cruised along at 20 mph toward the hospital, it struck me as depressing that the soundtrack for this long-awaited trip was pop hit (and super problematic) ear worm "Blurred Lines" by Robin Thicke.

Hey-hey-hey.

Before entering the hospital, my sister confiscated my overnight bag. She is a doctor, you see, and had some very useful insight. Apparently some hospital staffers get a little snooty when pregnant women arrive, packed and ready, like the hospital is a hotel.

"Hey—y'all got a room? I wanna have a baby, thanks."

Sister was right. I walked in (WITHOUT the bag), and I'll just say that my general experience with triage could be summed up in one sentence:

How can we kick you out of here?

Triage took my blood pressure four times. Three times it was through the roof, and the fourth time it was decent. So, obviously, the GOOD bp was noted on the chart.

I sat on a hospital bed and waited. And waited. I watched the little computer-graph-thing chart my contractions. As my abdomen coiled up like a snake, the numbers got higher and higher. Like watching a live-feed roller coaster of pain—whee!

The doctor called. Because I was one day shy of thirty-nine weeks, she wanted me to go walk for two hours. Like, "Hey, Mama—take a hike. Literally."

My sister's head cocked sideways and she instantly responded, "Aw HAIL NAW!"

So there she went, fuming and ranting and marching to the admission desk. Me waddling after her. Ian jogging after me.

Hot. Mess.

Flash-forward to the walking trail in front of Winnie Palmer Hospital.

Look! There's MK!

Big as a house and moving like a duck with a hemorrhoid. Ian made friends with a homeless dude who was drunk on Irish Rose and showed off the catfish he'd caught for dinner.

Here's a tidbit of information for those of you who are pregnant or perhaps wondering how to know when labor is FOR REAL.

Real labor is the land where your sense of humor goes to die.

I remember seeing my husband and his homeless companion. I

remember stopping. And I vaguely remember my head spinning around twice as I screeched, "I AM TOO DANG PREGNANT FOR THIS! GET YOUR <clever use of poor language> OVER HERE!"

Mr. Catfisherman and Ian's friendship ended immediately. I felt bad about that. It could have been a beautiful thing.

Ninety minutes later, back in triage, my contractions were thirty-five seconds apart. Nobody was impressed, I suppose, so they suggested I go labor at home.

That was it. I melted into a snotty pile of ugly-faced sobs.

Ian tried to console me while simultaneously sharpening his battle-ax for the next staffer who graced our room. It took about thirty minutes for that person to arrive.

That sweet nurse walked in, took one look at our family circus, and spoke the most beautiful words I had ever heard:

"Would you like to have your baby tonight?"

UM, YES PLEASE.

The next thing I remember is sitting on the edge of the bed, staring at the face of an angel: my nurse anesthetist.

2:00 a.m.

I woke up in a panic. "IAN!"

"Oh my—are you okay? Is it time?"

WE ARE HAVING A BABY

"My LEG! It fell off the bed, and I can't pick it up!

4:00 a.m.

Meanwhile, back at the hotel, my sister woke up because her "spidey senses were tingling." So my family raced to the hospital and by four-thirty they walked into my room.

Warning: somewhat gross descriptions ahead.

My sister entered the room as I explained to the nurse how I felt.

"Well, it's like I reeeeally have to poop."

The look on my sister's face went from calm confidence to furious frenzy. She pointed a finger and shouted demands, "When's the last time my sister was checked?"

Four hours.

"But don't worry. The doctor will be in shortly," the nurse said.

Sister's eyes went red.

"Oh really? Is that shortly like in a few minutes or shortly as in three hours? Because last time she was coming SHORTLY, she was gossiping at the nurses' station!"

crickets

Here's something you should know about me. I'm a middle child and I'm all about keeping the peace—even if it costs me a comfortable child-birth. So, instead of appreciating Sister's Last Stand, I got pissed and yelled at her.

IF you have a sister, you understand that picking a fight with Big Sis (aka protector, aka biggest fan, aka your hero) is not how you want to start the delivery process. But that's exactly what I did.

Shortly thereafter, Crouching Tiger Hidden Doctor made her appearance. Having been warned of the dynamics awaiting her, she came in all sorority-like, making small talk with my family.

She was just SO sorry for the misunderstanding earlier and she didn't see them in the hallway or she would have said hi and BLAH-BLAH-BLAH—get this baby OUTTA me!

Here's where we fast-forward let's say, twenty-seven minutes to be exact.

Baby Ben enters the world with the most pathetic "waah" ever heard. It would have been comical if it wasn't so disconcerting. He was busy making puny "waahs" and getting cleaned up or whatever they do to babies in that moment when my sister snatched the suction bulb off the doctor's table and proceeded to save my baby's developing brain. Hidden Doctor didn't appreciate her table being intruded upon, but Sister didn't give two rips. Let's just say that, in the future, I'll probably fly to Alabama and let Sis handle the whole baby-coming-out part.

Two doctors + one table = awkward dynamic.

They handed me my sweet little bundle of joy, and tears were shed, and cameras clicked, and . . .

I'm not really sure because my head hit the pillow and—I'm ashamed to admit it—the first thing that crossed my mind was how badly I wanted a nap.

Some mommies experience joy, elation, and instant love the SECOND they lay eyes on their little one. I'll be completely candid and tell you that my primary emotion was confusion. I looked at that perfect little angel and couldn't really reconcile that he was mine. I just felt strangely separated from the whole thing.

Then I got my nap.

I awoke in the recovery room to the sound of Ian's voice and a crib rolling into the room. Daddy was bubbling with joy.

"We went to the nursery and had a bath and I brushed his hair and I picked out a little hat and and and . . . "

It was adorable. And it was in THAT moment—a few hours after delivery, my world shifted into focus.

I had a son. I had a family. I was a mom.

Whoa.

It's been one child, a few years, and 700 gray hairs since that day. Boy, do I have some hilarious stories to share. Some humiliating, some heartbreaking. All of them important to the development of me as a person, a mother, a Christian.

And I intend to share so many of those stories with you.

This story ends with a baby in a car seat.

Strapped securely in the back seat of Daddy's pickup truck. Me sitting next to my newborn son, fussing over his blanket, over the buckles, over his hat. Daddy checking the rearview mirror eight hundred times. Driving fifty miles below the speed limit, all of a sudden acutely aware that people are driving recklessly.

That ride home will forever be cherished in my memory. We got home, pulled the car seat out, took several proud pictures at the front door, and walked inside.

WE'VE BEEN GIVEN THIS INCREDIBLE STEWARDSHIP OVER THESE PRECIOUS LITTLE SOULS.

There we stood, a family of three. Me looking at baby, Ian looking at me—the three of us wide-eyed in the center of the den.

"Now what do we do?"

Spoiler alert: You can flip to the end of this book, and you won't find the answer to that question. And real talk? I don't think there is one. Perhaps that is the messy truth of motherhood. We've been given this incredible stewardship over these precious little souls, and we are all just a little shell-shocked by that truth. We are doing our best, flying by the seat of our pants, and we are terrified.

Well, good news, Mama.

You are not alone.

Heart Kids

WILD AT HEART KIDS

IT'S HARD TO EXPLAIN THE STRUGGLE I have with my older child. Even typing the word *struggle* makes me feel guilty because he's everything I hoped for in a son. He's rough-and-tumble. He's cuddles and mud. He's this fabulous, uncontainable ball of energy, buzzing around our house, filling our lives with laughter and noise and the occasional broken lamp. I know I'm lucky to be his mama.

But the truth is, sometimes the wild of his heart makes me tired —really tired. Bone tired.

I spend all day clashing with his strong will, iron against iron, until the sun goes down. Then I go to bed feeling like a worn-down nub of a human being. There aren't enough activities in the world to burn his candle down. We can build tree houses and pillow forts, make mud pies, play chase, and completely skip naps. And even then, putting that boy to bed is like putting a cat in bathwater. It's a pay-per-view-worthy event, *every single night*. He's just not tired.

Not even a little.

And worse? I can't figure out how to discipline this child. When I'm harsh, it backfires. When I give him an inch, he takes six miles. He is bruised knees and outside voices, ninety miles per hour, all day, every day. And I am two steps behind, huffing from the chase and yelling for the fiftieth time, "Get down from that *right now!*"

So many of our interactions are composed of frustration and noise. I establish a boundary; he crashes straight through it. We are in a constant tug-of-war for power, and most of the time, if I'm being honest, he's winning.

I feel like I'm the frayed rope of a tire swing, and he's swinging higher and faster and higher and faster and higher and . . .

It scares me to think I could break.

How can I continue to parent like this, when everything he does feels like rebellion?

What happens when my last bit of patience comes sloshing out of the cup I've been desperately trying to keep steady?

Yesterday morning, I prayed that God would give me what I need to love this kid well. I pleaded with Him to reconcile the gap between the loud and the quiet, the crazy and the calm.

"God, please, show me how to do this," I begged.

And later that evening, as I was scrolling through pictures of our recent vacation, I came across this:

Like an answer to a prayer, a thumbnail picture of my wild-hearted child. My boy, frolicking in the waves with the energy of a thousand suns. He is King Max. His world —our world—is where the wild things are. The day he was born, a royal rumpus began. And every day since, we've been trying to keep up with the party.

As I sat there staring at the fiery little soul captured in thumbnail photo, I felt a whisper in my heart—an answer to my morning prayer.

You see those ocean waves?

They are both beautiful and wild. They dance and crash and roar, and maybe, to you, it seems like chaos from the shore.

But if you are looking from Heaven, you would see: there is a quiet force at work.

From a distance, a gentle guide is constantly pulling, fighting, creating order among the waves.

The moon and the ocean.

The push and the pull.

Don't you see?

A mother and her son.

The day he was born,
a royal rumpus began.

In one picture, God reminded me that my job is simply to be there. Calm and consistent.

To oversee the chaos of the wild. Not to tame it, but to quietly pull it into order.

Mamas, we will never tame the sea. So let's go ahead and cut ourselves, and our babies, some slack.

There is a place in this world for the calm and the wild. There is a purpose for them both.

Today, I am going to take a step back. I will let the waves crash and appreciate the incredible beauty that exists within my wild-at-heart child.

A Mother's

Milestone

A MOTHER'S MILESTONE

THE DAY THOSE TWO PINK LINES APPEARED, I felt the world stop moving.

What would have otherwise been a normal Tuesday was suddenly overcome by a tsunami of joy, fear, and squealing family phone calls. My brain buzzed, and a giddy smile lingered on my face. I could hardly wait until my husband got home. He eventually walked through the door, exhausted after a fourteen-hour shift. I wanted to make it a special moment. Like those quaint videos people record where the perfect present is waiting on the table or a loved one is sent on a scavenger hunt.

Instead, I just stood there in my pajamas holding a pee stick, and the news exploded out of me.

He rubbed his eyes and yawned. "I'm sorry, what?"

"We are pregnant." That sounded weird. "I'm pregnant." That sounded terribly lonesome.

"Babe. *We are having a baby!*"

Suddenly, Ian was wide awake.

We celebrated, hugged, cried. We chatted about names and genders and nursery decorations. A whole world of possibilities had emerged.

When my head hit the pillow, my mind kept racing. The silence of the house was suffocating. How was my husband snoring? How was I seriously the only person awake, pondering this little miracle growing inside of me? My dreams of him were growing with him.

What color would his eyes be? I could imagine his laugh bubbling up to the ceiling. His first steps. College graduation. I closed my eyes and hoped that wave would carry me away into the Land of Nod.

Then, I was hit with the biggest question mark my heart had ever felt.

I sat straight up in the bed.

"Will I be a good parent?"

I prayed. I texted friends. I googled articles, read message boards, and bought a few books on Amazon. None gave me the feedback I longed for. The affirmation that everything was going to be okay.

After a few days, I finally found "The App."

The App was this magical tile in my iPhone—this tiny little square I went to for all my pregnancy answers. It even tracked the progress of my growing baby.

I was a woman obsessed.

Milestones made me happy. Hour by hour, I received pings on everything from the ideal growth of my baby, to expected changes in my body, to birth preparation, and beyond. These milestones were clear indicators I was doing something right, so long as we stayed on plan.

ping Today your baby is an avocado! You should be eating more protein! Have you asked your doctor about a birthplace? It's important to talk to your avocado!

ping Today your baby is a squash! You should already be tracking Baby Squash's movements. Are you listening to Mozart?

PING! PING! PING!

This, my friends, was all before the birth.

Then came my son. He was angelic in every way. His soft skin, squeaky sounds, and milky smell—it was everything I ever dreamed of. But did I relish in his utter perfection?

No, not really. I mean, I tried.

But I was incredibly worried about his weak cry, crappy APGAR score, and poor latch. These were all tasks I needed to work on. Things I had to "fix" to be a good mother.

The next day, The App updated. It started telling me which

milestones this little human "probably" should be achieving, week by week.

Hooray! More things to monitor. I furiously checked boxes, proud that my son was ahead or on time for his milestones.

What makes a successful parent if not a successful child?

It was an exhausting roller coaster that left me frazzled and, frankly, insane.

A little while later, I was preparing for my son's eighteen-month pediatrician appointment, sneaking the bottle into the diaper bag like it was cocaine contraband. I couldn't possibly let my doctor see that Ben was still drinking from his "baba." That was definitely NOT on The App. But, two vaccines later, he started sobbing and pointing to the bag.

"Baba! Baba! Mama, pleeeeeaase!"

My doctor sat down on her stool and smiled. "You know, MK . . . it's okay if he has his bottle right now. He needs a little comfort."

She paused and waited for my reaction.

I was humiliated. I pulled my contraband bottle from the bag. He was instantly soothed.

"Ben is a happy child," she said. "He's loved, and he knows it. He's unafraid to try new things, and he's confident interacting with strangers.

All of that matters. Stop focusing so much on these milestones. I think it's driving you crazy."

She gave me a friendly, if not concerned, wink and left the room. In that moment, fear, pressure, and weight just emptied out of me.

Tears poured onto my son's little head until we were both exhausted and his bottle was empty.

The milestones didn't really matter.

All this time, I was tracking them for me. I needed to know if I was doing my job as a parent, and the only way I knew to determine my success was by his milestones. I needed to know if I measured up.

When I got home, I deleted that app. Instantly, I felt a weight float away.

I know now that I am a good parent, in every way that matters. That there are milestones—unwritten milestones—infinitely more important than a pincher grasp and potty training.

My child is loved.

He feels safe jumping from the side of the pool into my open arms.

He giggles at his own jokes, confident that his sense of humor is funny to others.

He runs to our bedside on stormy nights, knowing we will protect him from thunder and other scary things in the world.

When he scrapes his knees at the playground, he looks to me for the "am I okay or not?" response.

I watch my son's personality bloom and his sense of humor sharpen.

Those are the milestones no app can ever tell you. And believe me, they're the only ones worth measuring.

WHEN

Fear OF

Miscarriage
LOOMS

WHEN FEAR OF MISCARRIAGE LOOMS

DEAR SWEET BABY,

I announced your existence today. With a sweet picture of your daddy, mommy, and laughing big brother, we let the world in on a little secret. A blueberry-sized secret. A seven-weeks-along, maybe-it's-a-bit-early secret.

We are pregnant! Our second baby is in the works.

Friends told me I was crazy. "It's just so soon," they said.

They were worried because life is a little bit shaky this early on. Statistically speaking, your future is a bit . . . unsure. I could be glowing today, celebrating your growing little soul, and mourning your loss tomorrow. Miscarriage is real, and the possibility is looming.

For weeks, I let the fear of your loss into my heart. I let it silence me, quieting the joy of this coveted pregnancy. I let that fear snuff out the flame of excitement I had for you, until each night I spent waiting for the monster beneath my bed to pounce. I was nauseated, but refused to accept that was a "good sign." I had food aversions, but convinced myself it was "all in my head."

I was scared to accept you were here
for fear I might lose you.

I have friends and family who've experienced the roller coaster of pregnancy's joy and the grief of loss. It felt safer to stop hoping for you than it was to risk all that hurt.

So, the fear consumed me. I stopped discussing name possibilities. I stopped talking about nursery decorations. I stopped wondering how my other child would handle his "big brother" title.

I let the fear in, and it was making you disappear.

Then, on a Friday, you showed me your heartbeat. All it took was a few *thump-thump-thumps*, and I was head over heels.

Yes, it's early. Yes, it's scary. But it doesn't matter that I'm scared anymore. You are here *now*, and I want to celebrate every minute you exist.

Don't worry about those friends of ours—the ones who fear about it being too soon. They love me—and they love you, too. They are just concerned.

The truth is I was tired of being stuck in that holding pattern. All

that worry and fear was making you disappear—from my dreams, my joy, my hopes, and my plans.

What a tragedy that already was.

So today, I want to celebrate your life—tomorrow, too, and every day after. I want to celebrate the miracle that is you, for as long as your heart beats. Your presence is a gift that was prayed over.

And I choose to celebrate this gift as long as I have it.

Talk to your Kid

ABOUT BEING A

Weirdo

TALK TO YOUR KID ABOUT
BEING A WEIRDO

FIRST DAY OF KINDERGARTEN WAS SHOW-AND-TELL DAY at Blossomwood Elementary school, a sort of "get to know your class" activity. Letters went home to parents at the end of the summer, and kids returned to school carrying the most fascinating things.

Turtles, dried-out beehives, summer camp T-shirts . . . every child had an object and every object had a story.

That is, until a brown-eyed girl marched up to the front of the classroom empty-handed. The teacher seemed unsure, but the child smiled with excitement, so she shooed her along. Little feet stomped up cement block stairs to the center of the makeshift stage. She turned to face the classroom.

And that is when five-year-old Mary Katherine pulled her hands out of her pockets and pointed straight down at her girly-parts.

"Theeeeeeeese are my private parts!"

(Then, pointing to the class) "Yoooooooou *cannot* touch them!"

(Hands now on hips) "If you do, I will scream. And then I will dial 9-1-1. . . . Thank you."

And with a curtsy, I hopped off the stage and headed back to my desk, beaming with satisfaction.

The teacher handled things well, all things considered. After settling the classroom, she headed to the office and called my mother, laughing.

"Let's just say MK is *not* like her sister. She's definitely . . . different."

Different. A label that stuck for the next twenty-five years.

In kindergarten I didn't mind it so much. All a kid really cares about at that age is pizza and playgrounds. But some time, right around sixth grade, that label started to hurt. *I didn't want to be different.* I wanted to have shiny hair, an L.L.Bean jacket, and Express flare-cut jeans. I wanted to look and act like the popular girls in school.

I wanted to blend in. *To fit in.*

Because by the ripe old age of twelve, I had already discovered that sometimes being a standout means being a stand-alone.

And standing alone can get pretty lonely.

Well, my family couldn't afford designer brands. So off to middle

school I went, wearing combat boots and hand-me-down clothes. I walked through the double doors, whispering my mantra to the universe:

Different is cool. Different is cool. Different is cool.

By eighth grade, I had discovered pom-poms and popularity. I borrowed fancy clothes, rolled my hair, and smeared iridescent blue eyeshadow all over my eyelids. I was voted Best Dressed. I got myself a boyfriend. And at the pinnacle of it all, I managed to nab a lead role in the high school play.

Every night before the curtains rose, I felt sick. My stomach knotted up and I just kept thinking, "Nobody is going to buy this. I'm not this role. I'm not this person."

But each night I managed to get to curtain calls. Delivering the right lines. Feigning the right emotions.

Applause, curtains, rehearsal, repeat.

When the play was finally over, I was so relieved. I resumed my normal life.

Applause, curtains, rehearsal, repeat.

You see, even though the play was behind me, *my show* still had to go on. I curled my hair, grabbed my pom-poms, and took on the role I had been assigned. I was cool. I was popular.

I was miserable.

Let me tell you, friends. That's no way to live.

But how many of us have wasted entire seasons of our lives walking in the shoes of a stranger? Scared to be ourselves for fear of being isolated?

It's true that standing out can mean standing alone. But when it comes down to it, is there anything lonelier than being a stranger to yourself?

Let me answer that from experience: NO!

I finally quit my career as an actress. It just didn't suit me. Not as a person and certainly not as a parent.

You see, I learned that even though it is hard, it is okay to be a stand-alone. It's okay to let your freak flag fly. And even though they might struggle in the process, I want my children to know the same feeling.

I want them to know they are one-in-a-million

. . . not part of the crowd.

I want them to stomp out onto that makeshift stage of life with confidence and announce to the world that different is okay. Not only that, but *different is awesome.*

Time is a finite resource. And I wasted a whole lot of it being someone I didn't want to be. If I can save my children even one minute of an inauthentic existence, I will breathe a sigh of relief.

> WE WERE MADE TO SHINE. TO SURPRISE THE HECK OUT OF EACH OTHER. TO FREAK ONE ANOTHER OUT. WE WERE MADE TO BE WEIRD.

And you know what? I bet God will, too.

I mean, what do we think he's up there doing? Sitting on a throne with six cookie-cutter molds, punching out humans and sending us down to earth to be exactly like one another?

I don't think so.

We were made to shine. To surprise the heck out of each other. To freak one another out. We were made to be weird.

And I will tell my babies to do just that.

Yes, we should encourage our kids to be different. Even if that means other parents will talk. Even if that means that some of their teachers will stare. God made those babies exactly the way they are, quirks and all.

So you just smile, Mama, pat their butts, and whisper: "It's okay if they stare, baby. That means they are *watching*."

EVERY DAY I'M A

Mother

A LITTLE

Piece

OF ME *Dies*

EVERY DAY I'M A MOTHER,
A LITTLE PIECE OF ME DIES

I KNOW, THAT SOUNDS HORRIBLE. But please, hang with me. It's just . . .

Take for instance the moments when my son is in his highchair. I'm cleaning the floors and washing the dishes, and all of a sudden his arm magically transforms into a windshield wiper against the tray. Waffle bits and orange slices fly across the room. Just like that, rising up inside of me, is a piece of my heart that is angry and impatient.

And then I catch his eyes—bright and bubbling with laughter—and that angry little piece of me dies.

Then it's Saturday morning, and I'm comfortable in bed, and the sun is still sleeping. I think maybe, just maybe, I'll get a full night's sleep tonight. I hear coos. Then I hear squeals. Eventually loud cries are coming from the crib, and no, Daddy isn't making his move for the baby.

I roll over, frustrated, and a piece of me longs for the days when

weekends meant sleeping in until ten o'clock. My husband and I used to get tacos for brunch after sleeping in. Then we would go home and watch movies the rest of the day. Ugh.

I bet we never have a brunch date again. I stand up and shoot eye daggers at my still-snoring husband.

I walk into the nursery, and my daughter greets me by bouncing up and down, grinning her famous toothless grin. That's when I remember: mornings are her very best time. Mornings are when Holland tries new words and flirts with her mommy. As I lift her chunky, pillowy body out of the crib, she says my name in a tiny bell-like voice.

"Ma-Ma!"

In that moment, in that amazing freaking moment,
a piece of lazy longing just dies.

Then, I'm trying on clothes in Target's family dressing room, and my son's legs are swinging happily from the shopping cart. Nothing fits right these days, even though I've lost most of the baby weight. This boho tunic is looking a bit like a busted can of biscuits. I check the tag to see if it's a juniors large.

Nope.

Of course, a piece of me can't help whispering, "Before having kids you would have looked awesome in that dress . . ."

And it's true.

But I remember that skinnier, more fashionable version of me. She was a woman who desperately longed to find her soulmate and start a family. A woman whose hopes and dreams centered on the possibility of a life with children.

And then, after she'd been married nine years, faced trouble conceiving. And when she finally got pregnant with her son, pre-eclampsia loomed over his delivery. When that woman gave birth, that tiny little boy aspirated, and it was this woman's sister, the physician, who saved his life.

Yes, I remember that woman. She wouldn't give a crap about a few baby pounds. She was so grateful to be a mom.

I glance over at the beautiful boy who laughs in the Target shopping cart. He's so healthy and full of life . . . and all of a sudden it doesn't matter that the floral boho dress fits a little snug.

In that moment, a bratty, self-deprecating piece of me dies.

When nap time arrives, I'm soaking up the beautiful, coveted silence. A piece of my mind aches at the memory of unfettered independence. Of books on the couch and long, uninterrupted lunches. Of vacations that didn't require six suitcases. Of a simpler time and a quieter mind.

But then I recall my children's laughter. The sound of their little feet pitter-pattering across our kitchen floor. I think of all the beautiful chaos and noise that raising children has brought into my life. But I wonder now how empty my world would be without them. I realize I don't wish to know.

And suddenly, that rogue little ache, that selfish piece of me longing for any bit of quiet dies.

Motherhood is such a strange dichotomy. It is life-giving and exhausting. It constantly exercises my faith, tests my patience, and stretches my heart. But, as a result, my faith and patience are stronger. My heart is bigger. Although sometimes I still reach the end of my rope— my rope is getting longer.

It's true that every day I'm a mother, a little piece of me dies. But I will not mourn these losses.

My child is making me a better person every day.

And maybe, at some point, there was a piece of me that doubted whether or not having kids was worth the sacrifice.

But let me tell you, that piece of me has also died.

IT
LIKE?

WHAT'S IT LIKE?

I SAW HER, WITH THAT BIG OLE BELLY, smile at me and I could tell she had two hundred questions. She was thumbing through *Baby's First Year*, pausing occasionally to study certain sections.

We both stood in the parenting section of the local bookstore, each seeking our own answers. She with her pregnant belly and me with my grouchy toddler. I smiled back at her and returned my book to the shelf.

I ran my finger over a few more titles before deciding that there was no author on the planet with enough expertise to take on my family's brand of dysfunction. I had to succumb to the reality that we would be sleepless forever, and that was that. I huffed, reached down to pick up my kiddo, and headed for the door.

Grouchy Nugget wasn't having that, because I guess he had just in that second decided he was having fun, so he went full on limp noodle. I wasn't prepared for this maneuver, and his weight just about sent me reeling into the book shelf. I gave him my grittiest "try that again and you're gonna regret it" whisper, and as I grasped his arm to pull him toward the door, I just about walked straight into the belly of mama-to-be.

"So, what's it like?" she asked, warmly. Her expression was tentative and jubilant.

I had wondered that same question not so long ago when my belly and heart were stretched to the brink with life and potential.

But in that moment, when she asked, neither one of us was at our best. I was sleep deprived, and no amount of caffeine was clearing my brain fog. I had busted a button on my favorite pair of jeans that morning, and pretty sure Nugget had an ear infection. Which meant no nap for either of us. He was hungry and he was teething. The Orajel wasn't helping much. We were quite the pair, to be honest.

What is it like? Eep. I tried to divert.

"Huh? You mean . . . ?"

"Being a mom." She closed her book and set it back on the shelf, looking at me expectantly.

Surely she isn't looking to *me* for that answer.

Me, with the frazzled hair. With the wrinkled sweatshirt and baggy-butt jeans. With a kid wearing mismatched socks and—oh, no—is that cheese in his hair? Yep. Definitely cheese.

And we haven't even eaten cheese today. So . . .

She stood there waiting for a response, patient as can be. And I stood there, frantic, my mind racing away from me.

What's it like?

It's like . . . sore breasts and crusty eyes and not enough coffee in the world to clear the fog settling on your brain.

It's like the first night, when all the family helpers have left and you're finally home alone with your newborn. All those sleepless hours that you didn't think you'd make it through, but then the sun comes up, and you realize that somehow, by the grace of God, you did. A tiny seed of confidence is planted, and you think that maybe you can make it another night. Just maybe.

It's like baby's first boo-boo and you can't believe how much you panicked over one drop of blood. Your husband laughs because you cried more than the baby and now he's in trouble with you because it wasn't funny. It wasn't funny at all, and now you're punching your husband and crying even harder. What the heck has taken over your brain?

It's like a holy terror inside of you that harm could ever befall them. And a fierce warrior within you that would destroy anyone who dared try.

It's like the longest day ever and you've yawned four thousand times and can't wait for the kids to go to freaking bed. But then they melt in your arms, asleep in the rocking chair . . . and you just can't put them

down. So you stare. And stare. And . . . yawn . . . stare.

It's little feet and little meals and huge messes.

It's dreams of college and careers and weddings that you pray to be alive to witness . . . and the untold sacrifices you will happily make to secure those futures for your children.

It's too many feelings and not enough words to express them. From the very beginning, language falls short. That's what it's like. From day one.

Words fail.

Suddenly my heart was full. "You know," I said, "it's like nothing you can imagine or even prepare for. But you'll be ready."

It wasn't the best answer I had to give. But as she smiled at me and left, I hoped it was enough.

All I knew was she didn't need warnings. She didn't want my personal story.

What she needed was the assurance that she was ready.

And I could tell by the joy on her face and the way she nervously clutched her stack of parenting how-tos that she was.

One hundred percent.

in the
Laundry

CRYING IN THE LAUNDRY

HAVE YOU EVER CURLED UP IN A PILE OF LAUNDRY because it seemed like a good place to cry?

Have you ever sobbed in front of a mirror because you were in so much pain and you just wanted to be seen, but the only person around to share your suffering with was, well . . . yourself?

Have you ever hurt so deeply that you were certain your body would just stop functioning?

Have you ever cried until your eyes were swollen, your tears ran dry, and your face looked like it was stung by a hive of killer bees?

Have you ever let the shower run hot to cold as your shoulders shook with the inner sobs that no longer carried any sound?

If so, you aren't alone.

If not, well, this is awkward.

Here's the thing:

I have come to realize the depths of my biggest fears and the sting of my deepest pains are little more than fossils of my life's greatest beauty.

Maybe I'm sleep deprived. Maybe I need my meds adjusted. Or maybe it's just that sometimes life is truly hard, and I think we need to share these pains to normalize the fact that people suffer.

We all do.

And maybe it's good that we do, because I believe you can't truly enjoy the beauty of life if you haven't experienced the depths of its darkness.

Pain, you see, is the anchor of joy.

We can't have one without the other. Pain and joy are two sides of the exact same coin.

Don't believe me?

We are terrified of cancer because it makes us realize how fleeting and precious life is.

We fear for our children because we've never known love as deep as the love we harbor as parents.

We mourn a romantic breakup because we remember how beautiful love was before the fracture occurred.

We can't possibly feel the sting of want without the experience of wanting not.

We can't possibly know the valley of loss without once standing atop a mountain.

In short, there is no pain in this life that doesn't point to something beautiful that once was.

Pain is a fossil of beautiful things.

It's a footprint of something that left us.

And when we experience pain like this, friends, we have two choices:

We can let these ghosts haunt us, or we can turn them into our teachers.

As this is the eve of my bilateral mastectomy, I found my laundry pile tonight. A few months ago, I was diagnosed with breast cancer at the age of thirty-five. Right now, I am scared to death of the scars this surgery will leave on me, physically and emotionally.

Why did I never appreciate my body when it was healthy? Why did I not relish my feminine shape before it was altered forever by a surgeon's knife? Why did I feel so shy during intimacy, so embarrassed in a low-cut bathing suit, so ashamed in a formal gown that made me look buxom?

Today, I ache with sadness over the changes my body will experience. But when I wake up, get through this pain, and heal . . . I can make you a promise: I will do better.

This pain I'm experiencing? I know it points to something beautiful, and I will find that beauty again.

I will love my body with abandon, relish my health, and allow myself to feel proud of what's left of my womanly figure.

My pain will no longer hold me captive.

My pain will become my teacher.

Friends, when you find yourself in the darkest times, remember this: you only know what darkness is because you've experienced light.

When you are low, low, low in the valley, let that remind you that you've scaled some incredible mountains in your time.

You'll scale them again.

Run your fingers across the scars on your heart and remember the beautiful things that once existed in each crevice.

Those are what makes life worth living.

Let lost romance remind you that love is worth chasing.

Let your sick body remind you that health is worth celebrating.

Let your broken friendships remind you how deeply you can love and connect with another person.

When you find yourself curled up in the fetal position in a pile of dirty laundry (literally or figuratively, maybe I'm alone here), just remember there is no hurt in your life that doesn't point to something beautiful.

Find that beauty, remember it, and cling to it like a cat on a curtain.

Beauty is coming for us again, my friends. Our hurts won't last forever.

All we need is a little grace, a little time.

And perhaps, a pile of laundry.

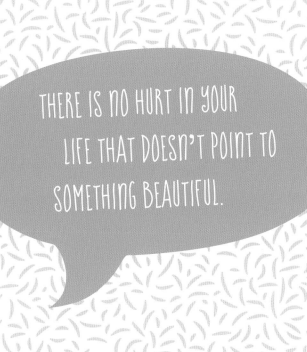

Dead

BIRD

DUH-DUH-DEAD BIRD

SOMETIMES I SHARE STORIES WITH Y'ALL THAT ARE POETIC AND HEARTFELT. Stories such as my kids playing in the ocean while I'm watching with tears in my eyes. Then I share some deep, existential thought on Christian spirituality . . . and those stories are great.

But this is not one of those stories.

In fact, the only reason I'm sharing this with you is in the event you have one of those particularly rough mornings getting your kids out of the door for school. You know the kind. Everyone's screaming, lunchboxes are forgotten, and you are minutes late getting in the minivan. You scream, *"Just buckle up and be quiet!"* The kids do, and just when they start sniffling, the gas light comes on.

This scenario only happens hypothetically, of course.

And if you've ever had a morning like that and you find yourself thinking "I am just a failure as a mother," I want you to stop right there and listen. I have a feeling my morning can make you feel a little bit better about yourself.

Seriously.

You see, every Wednesday, my son's preschool has show-and-tell to work on the "letter of the week."

Last week, for example, the letter was *H*.

Nugget brought a headlamp to school.

"This is my HEADlamp. Huh-huh-headlamp."

You get the picture.

Now, I'm not the most organized mom in the world. So this morning, I woke up like: "Oh crap, it's Wednesday! What's the letter of the week?"

scrambles through paperwork

"Nugget, quick! Go find something that starts with the letter D. Like duh-duh-DEE. Go!"

Nugget came back rather quickly with his favorite Spider-Man umbrella.

"How about dis umbrella?"

Uh . . . no, kid.

"Umbrella starts with the letter U. Uh-uh-umbrella."

He shakes his head vehemently.

"No, Mommy—DIS umbrella."

I'm trying not to pee my pants and embarrass him, and also I'm still hustling to pack his lunch, so I'm like, "Well that's pretty close, kiddo! But "this" is T-H. TH-TH-THIS."

Looking slightly dejected, Nugget sets his umbrella aside.

"Try again, baby. The letter D. Like Duh-duh-DINOSAUR."

His eyes light up and he goes, "Oooooh! Let me outside, Mommy. I know just the thing!"

Now pause.

This is where I tell you that for the last three days, I've been complaining that our porch smells horrible. And my husband has nodded his head like, "Uh-huh. Right. Smelling things again, honey?"

Which is also how he denies his farts, but anyway . . .

We go outside and Nugget immediately runs to his secret chair where he keeps his "collection"—rocks, bugs, that kind of thing. You know how kids are.

He points down and exclaims: "How 'bout my dead bird! Duh-duh-dead bird!"

He's reaching, while I'm screaming and dry heaving.

"*Oh mah gosh, son, don't touch it! Have you touched it? How long have you had this?*"

I am ready to bleach everything in sight, including my son and his bloated dead bird. Now we are late for preschool and still have nothing to bring for show-and-tell.

"Go get your doggy. Duh-duh-DOGGY. Go inside and get a stuffed doggy right now. Make it quick."

He ran inside with his mouth all twisty because I am the worst mother ever for saying he can't bring a bird corpse to preschool for show-and-tell.

I fling the dead bird over the fence, gag, and wonder what the heck else is in this collection when he returns, carrying something fluffy.

"Mommy, how about dis animal?"

I breathe in deep. It's either a dog or a cat, but who cares—it isn't rotting flesh, so I approve his selection and off to preschool we go. Twenty minutes late.

The letter D, y'all.

DUH-DUH-DEE.

As in today, Mommy is DUH-DUH-DONE.

(See? I told you you'd feel better.)

Overload

MENTAL OVERLOAD

"Whatcha thinking about, honey?"

I paused for just a minute, weighing the necessity of answering my husband's question fully, versus offering my typical answer, which would move the conversation along and keep everything comfortably casual.

"Nothing much, really," I said.

Which was a lie.

So I added, "Wondering how the kids are doing at the grandparents."

Which was less of a lie.

The truth is, like most mothers in this world, my brain is always spinning.

Always.

I couldn't tell you what I was thinking about the very moment he checked in, but the five minutes before he asked?

That hamster wheel was moving particularly fast.

About what?

Nothing. Everything. All the things in between . . .

"I need to pick up a new box of contacts before we leave town on Monday. Did I overpay the babysitter last week? My daughter isn't getting enough vegetables. I missed that writing deadline, again. Is this an anxiety issue? I should check in with my doctor . . . Which reminds me—does my son need any vaccines? I should call the pediatrician, pretty sure the preschool needs updated records. Did I register him for next year? Poor kid needs new clothes for school. He's grown so much."

Crap, the clothes. Forgot to switch the wash over to the dryer.

Note to self: Google recipes for baby-friendly veggies. Add to grocery list. Call doctor. Contact editor. Move wash to the dryer. But smell it first. May need rewashing . . .

"Man, I miss my little man. Can't wait to pick him up from the grandparents. Hope he's doing well today."

And that's exactly what I offered when he asked: the tip of the iceberg. Not because I can't tell him these things, but because . . .

Well, this is my brain. This is MOM brain.

All the time.

And apparently there's a name for this. The Mental Load, it's called.

It's why so many of us feel so tired. So, so tired, despite the fact that "all we do" is stay at home. And those of us who balance work, too? My goodness.

Have you ever seen a mom friend, asked her how she's doing, and she answered, "Tired."

It's not always sleep deprivation. Sometimes it is, but there's something else, isn't there? Something deeper.

My husband comes home from work, and I want to lighten his load. So I ask how his day was, because I care. And because I love him.

Because I love him and think the right thing to do is lighten his load, I listen to the details of his day. I take note of which colleagues are driving him crazy. I remember he mentioned that week in July he might have off, so I can check to see if there's an affordable condo available for a family vacation. He's telling me about his job, and I'm wondering if maybe he's trying to tell me we need to relocate, or if he resents moving to be closer to my family, or if maybe that comment he made about never getting a break means he needs space? No, that's not it. Oh, heck. Did he just say his boss's birthday is this Friday? What is an appropriate gift?

Always, in the back of my mind, the hamster wheel keeps spinning.

Mothers, you get this—right?

And it's not just relationship dynamics, either. It's . . . everything.

Because if we don't remember to switch the laundry over, who will? And if WE don't bother with the vegetables, well, the baby just won't get any. And doctors' appointments, prescription refills, vacation packing lists . . .

All on the invisible checklist inside our brain.

This is the mental load all moms carry.

And I'm not saying it's bad or that we need to do something to fix it.

I don't even know if we could.

But sometimes it's just enough to acknowledge that, hey, this exists. This is a thing. There's a reason we get tired even when we feel like nothing is getting done.

Everything that hasn't been done and everything that needs to be done is playing on a loop through our heads.

Mamas, we are incredible. We are freaking machines.

We are that fancy, expensive glue that's twenty dollars a bottle because it holds heavy stuff together while staying completely invisible.

But maybe we don't need to be.

How about the next time someone asks "What's on your mind?" you *tell* them.

Lighten your load.

And if they look at you like you fell out of the crazy tree and hit every branch on the way down, just own it. Talk about it. This phenomenon isn't going away if we don't admit it exists.

Listen to me: it is okay to share these things with your community. In fact, it's important to share these things.

The burden may be invisible, but it can get pretty darn heavy. Share the load. With your friends, your family, your church. With a therapist, if you find yourself sinking.

You can't be a good mama if you're sinking. You can't be a good wife, sister, or friend.

Most important, if you're sinking, you can't breathe.

Fight for your ability to breathe. Share the mental load, Mama.

You owe it to yourself.

OUT OF

Gas

AND

in need of

Grace

OUT OF GAS AND
IN NEED OF GRACE

IT WAS ACTUALLY KIND OF FUNNY TO WATCH, in a mean way. The white Lexus SUV sputtered to a stop about one mile from the gas station, and the driver absolutely lost his mind. He jumped out of the car in a slick, cream suit and proceeded to kick the tires. His hands flailed around as obscenities poured from his mouth. He grabbed his phone to send an angry text, or maybe an SOS. Then he proceeded to throw the phone into the grass.

He spent the next few minutes shouting, swearing, and cursing the earth. And then, just like that, he stopped. He found his phone, shut the door, and locked up the car. As vehicles whizzed by, his shoulders slumped forward and he walked. Down the hill, toward the Chevron.

Out of gas. Sucks pretty bad.

Some weeks, Mamas, you will be the shiny white Lexus and simply run out of fuel. If you haven't experienced it yet, don't worry, it's coming.

Perhaps you already know the feeling. You are cruising along with the windows rolled down, radio up. Or perhaps in a more parent-life scenario, you are busy sharing pictures of your sweet little kids, boasting about the wonderful time you've had on a beautiful beach vacation. Maybe you are sharing couples' pictures of you and your spouse with the caption "love this man sooo much!" You are putting out into the universe how much you love your awesome, awesome life.

Life keeps moving along. It all looks good,

feels good, is good. Until it isn't.

Something unexpected happens.

Maybe it's not a big deal, but it feels big. Like your kid is the biter in preschool. Okay, there are worse things in the world. Maybe the pictures of your vacation didn't represent reality. Maybe it rained the whole time and the kiddos screamed for eight hours on the car ride home. Then, you and your husband got in a fight when you finally got the kids to bed. You were crying when you uploaded those cute pictures to Facebook, because dang it—it just made you feel better.

Or maybe, your car really did sputter out on the side of the road unexpectedly. Maybe someone filed for divorce. Maybe a child got sick. Maybe you did.

Setbacks and disappointments are unexpected. You can't exactly schedule a "massive life breakdown."

Last year, my joy ride ended, and I was as shocked as anybody when the fumes dried up. There I was, stranded in a mess of my own making, with the shame of my seemingly perfect life exposed like a clunker on the side of the road.

I know this probably comes as a *huge* surprise, but my life isn't perfect. I'm in and out of church, my kids pitch fits in Publix, and my diet consists of toddler leftovers and ridiculously expensive lattes. Or maybe this doesn't surprise you, because you are human and you expect others to be, as well.

For whatever reason, I expect more from myself. My children need to sleep through the night, my house needs to be kept neat, and my waistline should be slimmer than a Kardashian's.

And for goodness sake, I'm a writer: I should be writing words.

But lately, at night, my kids wake up. My house is a wreck. My waist could be hiding a pregnancy or a dozen donuts. Who knows? I

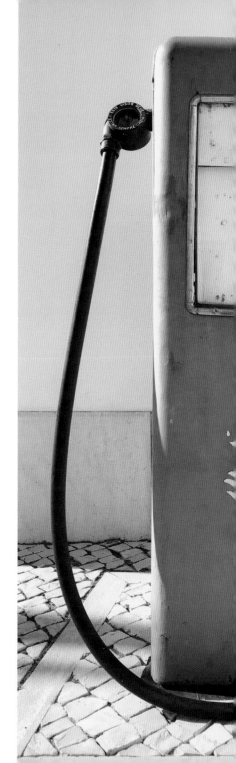

haven't been sleeping well, and I've been irritable with the people I love.

And despite all those warning signs, I never stopped to acknowledge that maybe—*just maybe*—my fuel light was on.

Today, I had to stop moving. Because today there was nothing left to make me move. I ran out of energy and laughter and encouragement. I ran out of patience and kindness and strength. It was both embarrassing and beautiful, because as it turns out—stopping was necessary for me to heal.

So now I'm on the shoulder of the road, assessing the problems that brought me to a stop.

I haven't taken time to rest. I haven't been seeking God and my spirit is yearning for his love. I have been digitally over-connected until my brain circuits got fried. I have been going and going and going . . .

When my entire being was yelling for me to *stop*.

And here's the thing. None of us can pour from an empty cup. What kind of parents could we expect ourselves to be, running on fumes while trying to herd cats? It's no wonder we end up with the occasional short fuse. We are empty. And we are in desperate need of fill-ups. So what do we do when we feel this way?

I can tell you what I do.

I stop. Today, I'm going to take the minutes, hours, or days it takes to recharge my heart. To energize my faith. To give and receive love from the people around me. To see clearly a world I've been zipping around, but not engaging in.

I'm out of gas, and it sucks pretty bad.

But it's not hopeless. As alone as I feel in this moment, I'm far from stranded. This is really just an inconvenience; I know that. So when I'm done throwing my hands around and cursing the ground, I'm gonna lock up shop. I'm gonna grab my little gas can. And I'm gonna walk the hill toward the source of my strength. It may be a bit of a hike, but I know the way.

I'll get there.

"Come to me, all you who are struggling hard and carrying heavy loads, and I will give you rest. Put on my yoke, and learn from me. I am gentle and humble. And you will find rest for yourselves. My yoke is easy to bear, and my burden is light."

Matthew 11: 28–30

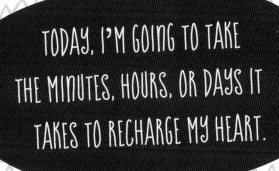

THE Playground

HATE IS ON THE PLAYGROUND

WHEN I WAS IN FIFTH GRADE, I STARTED A CLUB BY THE SWING SET. Every day at recess, we would do cheerleading dances. For fifteen minutes between snack and lunch, we were the jumping, dancing Cat's Pajamas.

It was really quite exclusive.

The group got so popular we decided to have tryouts. The space by the swings was getting crowded, and after all, what's the fun of a club if *everyone* is invited?

I remember a black classmate (whom we will call Casey) who showed up to those recess tryouts. She could jump and yell. She had a beautiful smile.

So I thought to myself, *Casey belongs in our club!*

But another girl informed me that Casey couldn't be in our club because the smell of her hair "bothered" other people. She was different from us. And because children are easily persuaded—or perhaps because

there was *already* a shadow of prejudice forming over my very young heart—I agreed and took Casey's name off the list.

I saw her crying in class the next day, and I didn't have to wonder why. My spirit screamed *this was wrong!* So I passed a note to my friend asking if she thought we had made a mistake.

"Does Casey's hair *really* bother you? Are you sure it isn't something else?"

And the teacher picked it up.

My teacher was a black woman who always dressed to the nines and swung her AKA keychain around her finger.

"What's AKA?" I once asked.

"It's a special club," she responded.

"Can I be in your club?" I asked.

"Yes." She would always affirm me.

I knew my teacher was going to be disappointed when she read that note, and she was. She pulled me aside after class, and before she could get the words out of her mouth, I began sobbing.

HATE IS HATE.
AND SADLY, HURT IS HURT.

"I just wanted everyone to be happy!" I confessed.

I felt that point was important because it totally justified my actions.

"Well, MK . . . was everyone happy?"

"No. Casey was definitely not happy."

"And who else wasn't happy?"

It turns out, I wasn't happy.

I was in fifth grade when I learned that happiness at the expense of another isn't true happiness at all. I still get a knot in my stomach, wondering what kind of life lesson was imparted to a sweet young girl who only wanted to dance with the other cheerleaders. It doesn't matter that we were "just children."

Mean is mean.

No. *Hate is hate.*

And sadly, hurt is hurt.

I am so deeply ashamed and sorry for my actions, and I can only hope that event didn't alter Casey in any significant way. But I know it altered me.

I share this humbling story today in hopes that it reminds us, the parents, of the consequential task we have at hand.

It's our job to raise the includers. The advocates.
The openhearted. The *kind* ones.

It's our job to talk to our children about racism, about sexism, about *all* the "isms."

It's our job to teach our children how to love different people without pretending those differences don't exist.

What we model in our homes will be replicated by tiny people with very big feelings.

So, today I ask: how are our children playing?

In the blink of an eye, those playgrounds will become our society.

We should want to send children into this world who are better than us: kinder, more inclusive, and more aware.

But that starts right now, with us, the parents.

It starts with me, and with saying:

I was wrong, and I am sorry.

One
Thousand

TINY

Breakups

ONE THOUSAND
TINY BREAKUPS

I never wanted to be *THAT MOM.*

The one who laments that every childhood phase is happening too quickly. Who waxes nostalgic with every single milestone. The hot, blubbering mess at preschool graduation. I'm not her.

But nobody warned me about these little breakups.

It was a blue-sky day in Hilton Head, South Carolina. My little family headed to the beach, towing Nugget along in his Radio Flyer. We were Instagram worthy, I'm not even gonna lie. A perfect picture.

When we arrived, I unbuckled my son and lifted him from the wagon.

And in that perfect picturesque moment, my little man yanked his arms away from me and leaned back.

"No!" he protested.

Baffled, I paused. Then I reached again to lift him up.

"No!" He squirmed as I pulled him out of his seat. "Get down!"

I sat my little buddy down on the sand and reached for his hand with my finger. (Maybe he didn't want to be held?)

"No, Mama!" Nugget declared, turning toward his father. He toddled away, reached for my husband's hand, and turned back with a wave.

"Bye-bye."

My son wanted me to stay behind. He wanted to be alone with his daddy. It was actually pretty sweet.

So why, then, did my heart ache?

It was a shadow of former heartbreaks, but the feeling was

nonetheless familiar. The forced space. The verbal dismissal. It was the first time as a mother that my child actually rejected my company.

Hello, breakup. We meet again.

I waved my boys along and sat on a towel to pretend-read a magazine. I pulled my sunglasses down and my magazine up. Nobody was gonna see me cry.

I'm not that mom, remember?

My husband and son played in the waves. Nugget picked up some shells, ate a little sand, and returned to the wagon for a cruise beside the dunes.

But I wasn't in the present. My mind raced away from me. I saw, for the first time, a heartbreaking peek of what motherhood had in store: **one thousand tiny breakups.**

I saw my son shooing me away from the bus stop. "Mom, I know where to go. Can you just wait here today?"

I saw him picking out his own clothes: a Ninja Turtle T-shirt and mismatched socks. "Mom, I can dress myself. I don't need your help anymore, okay?"

I saw a dejected basketball player on the ride home from a middle school game. "Mom, I'd really like it if you didn't cheer so loud. The other guys make fun of me."

First cars and first dates and high school graduation. A college bumper sticker on a trunk packed full of blue jeans and tennis shoes.

"Don't worry, Mom. I'll be home by Christmas."

I could practically feel that little Nugget wave.

"Bye-bye."

I know now that parenting is the process of raising someone up just to let them go. And maybe it's a small grace that it doesn't happen all at once. I don't think my heart could take it.

It's a mother's highest hope that her children find happiness in this world. That they grow in confidence toward a life of independence and fulfillment.

But that doesn't stop the process from hurting.

My son will never need me more than the day he was born. And tomorrow, if I'm doing my job, he will need me a little less.

There are a thousand tiny breakups between now and the day my son is fully grown.

And I do believe I will allow myself to feel some of this sadness.

Because, if I'm being entirely honest, maybe I am "that mom."

And this childhood thing is happening way too fast.

You Can Have It All,

JUST *Not All* AT ONCE

YOU CAN HAVE IT ALL,
JUST NOT ALL AT ONCE

I LEFT THE BEST JOB I EVER HAD TO BECOME A STAY-AT-HOME MOM. It was a tough decision. I hadn't finished my degree, so my journey up the corporate ladder looked an awful lot like a cat climbing a tree. When I finished packing up my desk, I stole one last glance from that penthouse window overlooking a lake. Ten years of claws-out determination, and I was headed home for the unforeseeable future.

Goodbye, career.

That Saturday night, I scrubbed the sleep from my eyes and pulled on a poor-fitting dress. Postpartum weight had settled in all the strangest places. Spanx only made me feel like a busted can of biscuits.

Ugh.

I straightened my hair, caked on some eyeliner, and wrote an insanely long list of instructions for the babysitter, especially since our boy pretty much just drank bottles and slept. With a gift card to Olive Garden, my husband and I headed out for a "celebration" dinner. I was no longer a working woman. *Hooray, or something.*

I was exhausted and so was he. We hardly talked. Conversation circled around our newborn, even though we were supposed to be "getting away for a while."

Finally, over a plate of congealed noodles, we quit trying for normal conversation and pulled out our phones. Scrolling through baby pictures, my husband took my hand. He looked deeply into my eyes in a way that caused my heart to flutter.

"We did something really amazing, didn't we?"

We really did.

♥

A while later, I sat on the couch drinking coffee. Nugget bounced in his Einstein toy and another episode of *The Good Wife* started up.

I felt regret creeping in. I was sick to death of soap operas, breast pumps, and pajama pants. I longed for pearls, adult conversations, and my window overlooking the lake.

But right that moment, my son stopped bouncing and lifted a pudgy finger.

"LUB YOU!" he declared, beaming with satisfaction and pointing at me.

My heart nearly burst.

You can't have it all, they say. But I have to disagree. You can have it all, just not all at once.

Happiness is not a cup that is empty or full; it is more like a puzzle. There's a whole lot of treasure in the "right now" in this world, scattered around you, waiting to be discovered.

I had a career-shaped hole in my life that has now been filled.

A love-shaped space that my spouse fits perfectly.

And there was a motherhood-shaped hole I didn't even know existed until my son arrived to fill it.

With each day, the world offers new joys buried beneath the mundane like a coin under the sand. Wonderful to discover, but sometimes hard to see.

Some days I wonder if my career days are forever behind me . . . if I'll ever have the satisfaction of a hard-earned paycheck, or if my business skills will ever again be put to good use.

But I've had that wonderful career. I've felt appreciated and challenged.

At times, my husband drives me crazy . . . when I feel unappreciated or even angry. Days when I find his socks and remnants of his snacks scattered throughout our house.

But even on those days, I know I have a marriage worth fighting for. I know I have a parenting partner I can fully trust.

I experience days when I'm exhausted and the dishes pile up, when my eyes burn and my head hurts from lack of sleep.

But even on those days . . . I can thank God for two beautiful children whose souls are blooming right before my eyes. Who are here, with me, healthy and alive.

We cannot predict the whole picture of our lives. We are ants on a tapestry, wondering where a single thread leads.

This life is a work in progress. And so, it seems, is our happiness.

And though the big picture remains unclear, I'm confident that at the end of life, I'll look back on parenthood with a smile. I'll see the way the puzzle came together and realize that I did, in fact, have it all.

Maybe not all at once. But instead . . .

A.

Little.

Bit.

At.

A.

Time.

YOU CAN'T HAVE IT ALL, THEY SAY. BUT I HAVE TO DISAGREE. YOU CAN HAVE IT ALL, JUST NOT ALL AT ONCE.

I

Really

Miss THAT

I REALLY MISS THAT

A TIRED, NEW MOTHER WEARS HER BABY through the aisles of Target, hair in a messy bun and eyes burning from sleep deprivation. She pauses briefly to pull a stylish dress from a discount rack, wondering if the flowy ruffles would conceal her postpartum pudge.

Twenty-five dollars is a lot of money, she thinks, placing the frock back with a frown. Then, she hears the giggles of two women. She watches as they mindlessly shop the same section with fresh makeup and smiles. Their carts are loaded as they turn to the dressing room, hot lattes in hand. A pang of envy sneaks into her gut.

"I really miss that," she whispers, pushing her cart toward the diaper aisle, kissing the hair of her snoozing infant.

A woman walks through the sale racks, grabbing items and tossing them into the shopping cart. As grateful as she is that her best friend flew in from out of state, all she really wants is to be home beneath the covers. This is supposed to be an outing to "get her mind off the pain." But everywhere she looks are mamas with babies or growing bellies. She takes a sip of her chestnut latte and throws a beige leather purse into her cart, pushing back tears.

Her hand wanders down to the place a baby once grew. Oh, how she longs for a kick in her belly, or any proof of the growing life that once existed inside. Her eyes wander toward a tired new mama, kissing her baby's head and strolling toward the diaper aisle.

I really miss that, she thinks, heading to the dressing room with her friend.

A teenager rolls her eyes and huffs loudly. "Mom, they wouldn't sell it in the JUNIORS section if it was inappropriate for my age. Gahd, I don't know why you are so ridiculous about this. I can't wear anything that's cool!" Her mother hesitantly eyes the floral halter top, inspecting its spaghetti straps and short-length waist. "Honey, if it was just a little bit longer . . . " Her voice trails off as her daughter storms away.

She pushes the cart after her, throwing the flowery halter into the basket. As she follows behind the angry teen, she hears a toddler squeal with delight. She smiles and watches as the toddler's mother lifts him out of the shopping cart and nuzzles him close for a hug.

I really miss that, she thinks.

Toddler mama nuzzles her little man with a hug. After months of teething and sleep-deprivation, she was beginning to feel defeated. But last night Little Man slept seven hours. Seven. Whole. Hours. She felt somewhat human after a ginormous coffee and a frantic, two-minute shower. One good day almost wipes out the memory of a hundred bad ones. Maybe, just maybe, they were turning a corner. She places her son, with a kiss, back into the cart and heads toward checkout.

Thank God for one. Good. Day.

The little old lady with powder-gray hair fumbles for the Target dog sticker when she sees a young mom approach the register. Sixty years of hard work, and she still can't find it in herself to retire. Her joints ache from standing and scanning, but she still finds joy in the interactions she would otherwise not have in her quiet, dusky apartment.

She offers the young mom a receipt and a sticker to the toddler. She blows kisses to the bouncy boy. He giggles in return.

She smiles at the next woman in line with a full cart. "What a lovely purse you found! It will work with every season!"

She gives a knowing wink to the mother with a teenager, whose pouty-lipped daughter has her arms crossed (Mom decided against the

Thank God for one. Good. Day.

floral halter, after all). The sweet old lady hands the receipt to Mom, then addresses her daughter.

"Thank God for every day you have your mother. I lost mine twenty years ago, and not a day goes by that I don't miss the chance to argue with her."

As the teenager rolls her eyes and mumbles "Yes, ma'am," the elderly woman closes her checkout lane and clocks out for break.

With tears gathering in her eyes, and memories flooding her mind, she quietly whispers: "I really miss that."

toenails

PINK TOENAILS

I WAS TWO MONTHS POSTPARTUM the day I finally got out of the house with my second-born child for a little mother/daughter time. After lunch, I found myself sitting in the lobby of my favorite nail salon, waiting to pay for a set of pink toenails. The morning had been a grand success and frankly, I was feeling pretty darn good about life.

My much-needed pedicure had been a quiet, enjoyable experience. Baby Holland spent the whole time snoozing against my chest in her carrier, happy as a clam. I kissed the top of her milky-sweet head a few times for good measure, then wiggled my pretty pink toes. The smell of fresh baby combined with a good old-fashioned pampering had me in a state of downright euphoria.

Nobody was gonna steal my sunshine today.

A little bell jingled as an older lady walked through the glass shop door. She took a seat across the room, and after a few moments I couldn't help feeling her gaze upon me. It practically burned. She cut her eyes, first to me, then to the nail shop owner, and then back to me. After a few moments of glaring, a sour, judgy look fell across her face.

"Aren't the fumes in this shop hurting that poor baby?" she blurted out, loudly.

Of course, she didn't bother asking me. Nope. Instead, she asked the nail shop owner while pointing in my general direction.

I was being called out. Judged. Shamed.

And she didn't even have the dignity to question my parenting choice to my face.

I wanted to open my mouth and say something. I don't even know what. So many words ran through my mind, and about as many feelings churned in my heart, but all of them just clumped right in the center of my stomach. Tears burned in the corner of my eyes.

Was I really a terrible mother? How had I made such a reckless choice without even realizing it? Had I made a mistake leaving the house with my young baby? Was I being selfish? Maybe I should have stayed home longer like I had with my first child. All I was trying to do was get a little sunshine and happiness. Was that really so wrong?

All of a sudden, my pink toenails didn't feel so pretty. I was flush full of shame. I wanted to vomit. I wanted to disappear.

I opened my mouth to defend myself, but words escaped me.

It's not very often that I'm rendered silent.

It was in that moment, when I needed one most, an angel in the form of the nail shop owner showed up. She shot me a reassuring look before turning her tiny little body and her full attention toward the blue-haired Judgy McJudgerson.

"If babies weren't welcome here, there would be a sign on the door saying 'NO BABIES.' But babies are welcome. If that's a problem for you, you should leave. This mama is welcome in my shop. This baby is welcome in my shop. And if you are worried about the fumes, perhaps you should hold your breath with your concern."

Ho. Lee. Crap. My eyes were wide as saucers.

The old woman's face puckered up like she had eaten a bad fish. She got squirmy and quiet in her massage chair, and I honestly don't know if she stayed for her pedicure or not. I didn't stick around long enough to find out. I paid my bill and tipped as generously as I could afford. I proclaimed that I'd be seeing them again—and soon.

Then I turned on my heels, with my pretty pink toenails, and left that nail salon, with my precious daughter in tow, the doorbell jingling behind me.

As I tucked Holland into her car seat, I said a silent prayer. I thanked God for the angel who intervened on my behalf that day, saving me from the shame that I know now I didn't deserve to feel.

We mothers wrestle with enough of that on our own, don't we? We struggle all the time with fear, shame, insecurity, and worry. Every day we doubt our abilities to do right by these precious little blessings. It's not like we need help from strangers in the grocery store. We feel outside pressures by society and family and magazines. Then we play the comparison game with our friends and colleagues. It's a never-ending and exhausting process of measuring ourselves against someone else's standard and constantly coming up short.

Let me tell you something, Mamas. That's no way for us to live.

When I had my first child, Benjamin, I was diagnosed with post-partum depression. I remember being terrified to even leave the house. Every snack choice was scrutinized, every outing was meticulously planned. I was convinced that every life choice would cataclysmically impact the direction of my infant's life. So, the easiest thing to do was play it safe: stay in the house, avoid public scrutiny, and hide from what I perceived to be danger and judgment.

Eventually I saw a doctor who—wouldn't you know it—recommended I get out more (not less).

It turns out, a healthier, happier mama
makes for a healthier, happier baby.

I took that advice to heart, and it changed my life.

YOU LISTEN TO ME RIGHT NOW, MAMAS: YOU SHOULD DO THE EXACT SAME THING.

If pink toenails and a little bit of sunshine are enough to cut through the fog of that newborn phase or combat those new baby blues, then that's exactly what your doctor ordered. You put that sweet little baby in a carrier right now and drive to the closest nail salon. Pick your favorite color. Lean back in that massage chair, snuggle your baby tight, and enjoy the luxury of freshly painted pink toenails.

Your happiness and your sanity matter.

And those blue-haired judgmental old hens can take a hike.

Theft
AUTO

GRAND THEFT AUTO

IT WAS A SATURDAY MORNING AND I WAS ON DAY FIVE OF SERIOUS SLEEP DEPRIVATION when I strolled into Starbucks, looking like a hungover zombie.

I ordered a triple venti crackuccino and stalked the counter waiting for my order. When the barista called my name, I swiped that cup and chugged it like a frat boy on a Saturday night. If you've ever done mornings with a toddler and a baby, you understand why this was necessary.

Aaaaaaaaaaah, caffeine.

When that first shot of espresso hit my bloodstream, the fog lifted. I was feeling less undead by the minute, so I figured it was time to put on my big girl panties and face the day.

No, better than that. I was ready to conquer my day!

Riding a caffeine high, I grabbed my keys and headed to the parking lot.

Get ready, world!

There my minivan sat, in its usual spot. I tugged the door open, mindlessly juggling a purse, my cup, and the half-spilled bevvy I picked up for my hubby, who was home with the kids. I plopped into the driver's seat and placed my drinks in the cup holders. I threw my purse on the floorboard and flipped open the mirror to check for chin hairs. I was bummed to discover an overhead light was out.

Huh. That stinks. Didn't even know that was possible . . .

Then I noticed that something smelled funny. I checked the seat behind me to see if I left yesterday's lunchbox in the sun to rot. This had happened before, but nope. No sign of lunchbox. Also, no sign of the second car seat.

Boy, that's weird. I could've sworn I had two kids this morning. *shrug*

Maybe it was how the sun streamed through the windows, but I started to wonder if I was seeing things. That leather interior sure looked . . . black. And mine is tan, right? Yeah, definitely tan.

I think.

Maybe I need more coffee. Or maybe I've had too much coffee.

Or—*uh oh*—maybe I'm finally going crazy.

I was beginning to panic, like one of those characters in a scary movie. You know, the one where strangers sneak into the house and make little changes? They move the coffee pot, switch a light off, and all the while the homeowner is going bonkers like, I swear I left that pot over there . . .

Yeah, that.

Strange smell. Missing car seat. Weird interior.

But, y'all, I got in this car with my keys. Right? I clicked the button and everything!

I grabbed the key, shoved it in the ignition, and turned it.

Nothing.

I tried again.

Nothing.

And that is when I noticed the wallet-sized picture taped to the dash.

Well, that kid was definitely adorable. And he was definitely my son's age.

But he was *definitely* not my son.

There were Mardi Gras beads dangling from the rearview mirror, and that is when it hit me.

Holy crap! This ain't my car.

This. Is. A. Stranger's. Car.

I was in their front seat! With the freaking door closed! I'm using their cup holders!

What was I supposed to do?

The obvious answer would be to get out of the car, and quickly.

Of course, that wasn't an option for me as I had just placed two Starbucks cups in the holders and thrown my purse on the floorboard, spilling half of its contents. I was freaking out, scrambling to put my purse back together and escape unseen.

Gum, in! Water bottle, in! Tampons, in! Sippy cup, in! Let's *get out!*

"Deliver me, Lord Jesus!"

I ducked out of the strange van and hustled across the parking lot, looking back over my shoulder every two steps like "act cool, act cool, act cool." I got to the spot where my identical minivan sat without being noticed by a single person.

Phew.

I balanced my cups on the hood of the van and dug around my purse for the keys and . . .

You guessed it.

By this time, the stranger was getting into her minivan, and I had to run over there and explain—this is the absolute most embarrassing thing ever—but "Hi, I was sitting in your van a minute ago on total accident and I was trying to go home, but I left my keys behind."

This is where it gets good.

Y'all, she laughed. Like genuine, hysterical laughter.

She totally saw me sitting in her car and couldn't decide whether to call the police or give it a minute to see how it played out. And lucky me (I think?), I got out of her car just seconds before she decided I was trying to steal it.

So help me, I just about went to jail for grand theft auto.

I am telling you right now, whenever I doubt how good the Lord is, active and able to work out the messes I keep making in my life, I remember that time sleep deprivation nearly landed me in the slammer.

Instead, I ended up with a good-humored new friend who has an adorable kid my age and excellent taste in minivans.

I got a double shot of grace that morning.

Some days just call for two. Amen?

Hurry

up,

rapunzel

HURRY UP, RAPUNZEL

A PIGGY-TAILED TODDLER STOOD ON HER TIPTOES in front of the Disney souvenir stand, brandishing a magic wand. Reaching out with the blinking plastic star, she smacked a stuffed mouse and giggled.

"Bibbidi, Bobbidi, BOO!"

Before said mouse could turn into a horse, I grabbed my daughter by a poufy-sleeved arm.

"Hurry up, Rapunzel! Cinderella isn't gonna wait!"

Unto my hip she went, and we power-walked to our Fast Pass appointment with Cinderella. Holland rested her head on my shoulder, keeping an eye on that stuffed mouse as long as she could.

Bibbidi-Bobbidi.

Later that day, at Animal Kingdom, our family stopped at the lion exhibit. The animals were less than thirty yards away, stretching and yawning from their perch on a boulder. Holland placed her little hands against the glass, leaned forward, and stared in awe. She watched as one of the lionesses began to clean herself. It wasn't too unlike the way our cat, Waffles, cleans himself at home.

Holland looked over her shoulder and flashed a wide grin.

"Meeeeeow!" she said, licking her hand. "Meeeeeow-meow-meoooow!"

She pawed a spit-covered hand across her face and purred.

I checked my watch. We had ten minutes till our next Fast Pass at The Lion King show, and I'd be danged if we missed a single magical second of that show.

"All right, Kitty Cat! Time to go! Simba isn't gonna wait!"

Into the stroller she went with a kick and a hiss.

Meow.

Honestly, that's how the entire day went. Me, rushing my daughter from whatever exhibit or bubble machine grabbed her attention. Her, furious that Mommy would pull her away when all she wanted to do was lick herself in front of the lion exhibit.

"Hurry up, Rapunzel! No time to waste!"

It was like herding a cat to a river.

I strolled my sleeping princess out of the park well before five o'clock that day. The whole affair was a blur of magic, sugar, and toddler melt-downs. In the end, Holland crashed thirty minutes before our final Fast Pass.

Back at the hotel, I laid her down, costume and all, on top of the hotel covers. I pulled off her shoes, covered her with her favorite baby blanket, and kissed her sweaty head. Then I did what I suspect most parents do when they get in bed at the end of the day at an exhausting theme park.

I went to sleep.

Ha, just kidding, I stayed up 'til midnight scrolling through pictures I'd taken that day.

It was an album chock full of magic. There we were, with Cinderella. Smiles were forced, but pretty dang cute. Maybe even Christmas card material, which is saying a lot in early July. The Lion King was a hit, and Holland was hilarious striking her "growling like a lion" pose in front of the character poster. It was all very posed, precious, and magical.

But swiping through the pictures of the day's happenings, there was one single thumbnail that brought tears to my eyes.

It wasn't posed, and it wasn't planned.

It was a candid of my wild little Rapunzel: pouf-sleeves and tennis shoes, marching independently toward a magical adventure of her own making. Her hand clasped the wand, while the stuffed animal cart was just out of sight from the picture's frame. I knew exactly what she had done next. I could practically hear her tiny voice and laughter bubbling up.

"Bibbidi, Bobbidi, BOO!"

My eyes grew blurry at the thought, and all of a sudden, six little words popped in my head.

Words that every parent, every adult, and every human thinks at certain times in life:

I wish time would slow down.

The day had been magical, but it was over before I knew it. And yeah, I know what everyone says: "Time flies when you are having fun."

But you know what else is true?

Time flies when you're in a hurry.

As parents, we do our best to plan memorable moments. To create and capture every picture-perfect memory we can. From the second our babies are born, we get this instinctual sense we are on the clock, and the panic sets in. There's an urgency to relish every second and every moment.

We want to make it all count.

But what if we are so busy trying to make it count that we are missing the forest for the trees? What if, in our efforts to bring our children through the world in a series of picture-perfect moments, we miss the moments when they stop and discover the magic for themselves?

It occurred to me as I laid in bed scrolling through Lion King pictures, that I had literally dragged my daughter away from watching one of God's greatest creatures . . . so she could watch people in costume pretend to be those same creatures.

"Hurry up, Holland. Come with me. That magic is over *here*!"

I was so busy hurrying her along to my next awesome plan that I neglected to remember: life's most magical moments are rarely the ones we have scheduled.

Let's be honest, Mamas. If you look back on life's most cherished memories, how many of them happened on a schedule?

(Spoiler alert: they don't.)

They happen right before school, when you are running late and the lunches aren't packed. They happen when you and your husband are in a fight, and suddenly your baby figures out a new word and his eyes twinkle with excitement. They happen when you're running through the parking lot with your arms full of groceries, and a monsoon unloads on the entire family. Then there's spontaneous puddle splashing and laughter, and the whole family sings songs, soaking wet on the car ride home.

The real magic happens when we least expect it.
It happens when our cameras aren't ready.

> LIFE'S MOST MAGICAL MOMENTS ARE RARELY THE ONES WE HAVE SCHEDULED.

And if we aren't careful, this magic could very well happen when we are distracted by the next place we are "supposed to be."

All those posed and perfect pictures in my Disney vacation album are adorable. But I'll never forget the feeling I got when I came upon the snapshot of my sweet little Rapunzel, exploring a world of her own making, magical wand in hand.

I only wish I could lean through that picture and whisper back in time to the mama who was so keen on rushing that princess around.

I know exactly what I'd say, too.

I'd tell her that magic is with her wherever she goes. There's no need to drive herself crazy.

So, slow down, Rapunzel. You're growing too fast. And slow down, Mama. This time doesn't last.

THE
Magic
OF

Slowing
DOWN

THE MAGIC OF SLOWING DOWN

I SCROLLED THROUGH PICTURES AGAIN THIS EVENING. It's become a late-night habit of mine, which, based on my recent coffee intake, is probably a bad one.

But, dang it, I find the most wonderful gems on my phone in the middle of the night. And is there anything more addictive than those chubby-cheeked, thigh-rolled, baby pictures?

I think not.

I'll be the first to admit, I take an absurd amount of pictures of my children. If the human race were wiped out and aliens came to earth to study our existence, they'd probably conclude that my family was some sort of earthly royalty—not only because of the absurd photo documentation of their existence but also because my daughter is literally dressed like a princess in half of our photos.

One would think with a couple hundred albums full of memories, it'd be impossible to treasure every picture. But let me tell you a little secret: every night I look back on the past years' memories, and suddenly, a snapshot that didn't carry so much weight at the time might now stop me in my tracks.

And that's exactly what happened to me last night, when I scrolled past a photo that I had always found precious, but not overly meaningful.

It's a snapshot of my toddler son, sitting cross-legged in the driveway on a wet mat, eating dry cereal with his grandfather. It was Trash Day, which in our house is a national holiday.

My son's grandfather, Pap Pap, had woken up early and detailed my husband's pickup truck. He's the kind of man who does things like that.

The floorboard mats were still damp, so he set them out to dry by our carport gate. Then he came inside and got Benjamin out of bed. Together they poured a bowl of Cheerios, walked to the carport, and took a seat on the mats.

They sat out there for what must've been ages, crunching dry cereal and watching big trucks circle our neighborhood like it was the greatest thing ever.

And in that moment, I guess it was.

Tonight, rediscovering this picture, I think I've realized something big: the difference between grandparents and parents.

Parents are so busy trying, trying, trying. We want the best for our children, so we try to make it happen. The best schools, the best homes, the best childhoods. We plan and we scheme, trying our hardest to create magical memories with our kids that they will forever cherish.

But what grandparents know is the magic is already present. It's all around us, just waiting to be enjoyed. We don't have to force beautiful moments to happen with our babies.

We just have to slow down long enough
to notice them and then soak them in.

This little thumbnail picture has me in tears. I have spent entire weekends dragging my son all around town trying to entertain him. We go to Target, playgrounds, friends' houses, and birthday parties. At the end of the day, he's exhausted.

Many of those days I realize he's tugging at my shirt, asking for my attention. Instead, I'm forging ahead to the next activity.

And all he wants is my time.

Parents, if only we would stop. If we could slow down. If we paid attention, we might discover that all the effort in the world can't compete with a bowl of Cheerios, some damp car mats, and a big truck.

And really, isn't that wonderful news?

Children are pretty simple.

But so, it turns out, is magic.

WHAT GRANDPARENTS KNOW
IS THE MAGIC IS ALREADY PRESENT.
IT'S ALL AROUND US, JUST WAITING
TO BE ENJOYED.

Happens

SHIFT HAPPENS

I THOUGHT ADULTHOOD WOULD BE EASY.

It was according to MASH, anyways. Do y'all remember that game? Back in the good old days when we all passed notes on actual pieces of paper during class? I was in sixth grade when I realized you could determine your entire future with a pencil, a sheet of paper, and a random number.

In MASH you would get issued a Mansion, Apartment, Shack, or House. You would marry one of your four favorite men, and you were issued a certain number of children and a job.

Easy peasy lemon squeezy.

You were off to adulthood!

No one talked about mortgages or life insurance or property taxes. No one was warning us that marriage is so hard, or how even the best relationships break your heart from time to time.

And yeah, the painstaking process of family planning? Ha. Mamas only wish we could circle a number on a sheet of paper. If only life were so easy.

Whoever knew starting a family would involve peeing on sticks, crying every twenty-ninth day of your cycle, and taking your temperature in the most uncomfortable of ways—all for the joy of having a baby (or two or three)?

To say nothing at all of childbirth.

Yeah, I used to think adulthood was going to be simple. Now I realize . . .

Growing up is hard. So hard.

As soon as you think you've unlocked the next level of adulthood or figured this whole thing out, well . . .

Shift happens.

You lose your job.

Your marriage that was a rock yesterday is now just rocky.

You experience a miscarriage.

Or you never conceive at all.

Your house payment becomes an unbearable burden.

Or a parent gets sick.

You gain fifty pounds and no longer love yourself.

One day, the world is blue skies and sunshine. You've struck gold in MASH, and you set out on your great adventure. It all looks so easy, and you start to get cocky.

You think you have this parenting thing figured out, this finances thing figured out, and this life thing figured out. And then . . .

More shift happens.

The finish line is moved a little further away, and you are left standing alone, baffled. You want to cry or scream or throw something.

"Excuse me, this isn't how my game was supposed to play out!"

No, nobody told us that being an adult was so dang hard. Nobody told us we would have days we'd want to cry on the couch like children, call our moms, and relinquish control of everything—if only for a few hours.

But, we can't. Because we aren't those kids anymore.

Shift happened.

We are the moms of our homes now. Our babies depend on us. If bills are going to get paid, we have to pay them. If marriages are going to mend, we have to mend them. We don't get to play MASH and magically end up with the life we always wanted.

It's all work and grit and tears.

When you ache from the sting of life's loss, there is a powerful strength that comes with the healing.

It's difficult. It's exhausting.

But can I tell you something I've realized? There is still beauty in it.

When you feel a distance between you and your spouse, that's when a bridge gets built. When you lose your job and feel lost in limbo, that's the blank slate you never knew you needed. You get to grab your pen and start writing.

When you ache from the sting of life's loss, there is a powerful strength that comes with the healing.

You will find that these hard days—the ones that shift everything around—are the ones that reveal who you are.

Who you wanted to be. And that's what it is to grow up.

I know sometimes it feels like the moment you have life figured out, the rug gets pulled out from under you again.

But have faith in this:

You will be made stronger in the hardest of times. You will discover more about who you are with the change of every season. With every struggle, every hard day, every gray hair.

You are growing up.

If there's one thing I've learned in the last decade, it's that you can't get too comfortable where you are.

Because shift happens.

And even though life is scarier and harder and more discombobulating than we ever imagined . . .

It's still good.

It's hard, and it sure ain't MASH.

But it's good.

you won't **Know,**

BUT

I Will

YOU WON'T KNOW, BUT I WILL

"MOMMY, COME WITH ME? MOMMY, NO LEAVE."

I put on your tiny shoes, and your hand reached up to hold mine. We pulled your blue doggy backpack over your shoulders, and I smiled reassuringly . . . but my heart frowned. In the parking lot of your new preschool, tears were already in your eyes. Your feet shuffled toward your classroom, and you gripped my finger like a vise. Your lips turned down.

If this is a good thing, why does it feel so hard?

At drop-off you reached out your arms and cried my name. Big ole tears streamed down red cheeks. I gave you a kiss and walked back to my car, literally turning my back on your cries. The whole thing wrecked me. I wish you were old enough to understand why—but at two years old, you aren't. You've already gone back inside with your friends. You've probably stopped crying. I'm just getting started.

While these feelings are fresh and achy in my heart, I sit in the car, writing you a letter. Because when you get older—when you can finally understand—there is something I want you to know about preschool drop-off:

My sweet boy,

By the time you are able to read this, these preschool drop-offs will be a distant memory. Truth be told, you probably won't remember them at all. You won't remember the screaming or the tears or the way your teacher calmly held you as I hurried my way back to the car (in case I lost courage and ripped you away from their arms). You won't remember the panic on my face or the redness in your cheeks. *You won't remember, but I promise I will.*

You won't know how Daddy and I agonized over which preschool would enrich you, protect you, and encourage you to grow. How it took us six months in our new town to finally gain the courage to sign up. How after visiting twelve schools— twelve!—we settled at a quaint little preschool with colorful paper on every wall. The teachers were all so kind and had been there for years. We wanted you to trust these adults. To make new friends and play in confidence without Mommy hovering nearby. You'll never know how we fretted over this decision, losing sleep and tears. *You couldn't possibly remember, but your parents certainly will.*

You won't know how guilty I felt at home, cleaning the carpet for the third time. How the dishes were done, the bed was made, and how I was certain that by ten o'clock, your confidence in me was officially crushed. While you were wondering where Mommy was, I was on the phone with Ms. Joanna getting an update on how you played with that brown plastic donut and laughed when the teacher blew bubbles during circle time. You couldn't possibly remember these details. But sweet boy, know that I will.

Maybe you'll be seven years old when you read this, rolling your eyes because this letter only proves how ridiculous Mom truly is. Maybe you'll be a teenager, embarrassed by this emotional train wreck of a confession. Or maybe, I like to imagine, you'll be packing up a safe four-door sedan with blue jeans and polo shirts. There will be a college bumper sticker on the back, a tank full of gas, and you will smile at me as I grip your hand like a vise.

And maybe, as you pull out of the driveway, you'll find this letter folded neatly in the passenger seat.

There will come a day when Mommy is the one at drop-off. Perhaps I'll put on a brave face. Or there will be big tears streaming down red cheeks. Either way, it will be your turn to hurry back to your car and leave me sniffling in the rearview. And when that moment comes, you'll be looking ahead to some new adventure—not looking back.

You'll be looking ahead to some new adventure — not looking back.

You won't be remembering the lunch boxes, the tiny socks, or your 2T Mickey Mouse T-shirt. You won't know I woke up an hour early today so we could make wildberry muffins before preschool. You won't know that I dropped you off on that first day and sat in the car to write this letter (while sobbing like an idiot). You won't know all the pride and love and joy and sadness that simultaneously consumes parents' hearts when they see their child take a step—or leap—toward independence.

And you won't know how that feels.

But perhaps someday there will be another pair of hazel eyes staring up at you. A tiny hand squeezing yours, in a red-and-teal-striped blanket. You will cuddle that tiny body close and deeply inhale the sweetness of a newborn baby's hair. And all of a sudden, you'll feel a wave of magic rush through your bones. The scary, unrelenting, irrevocable love that comes with being a parent. You will whisper "I love you" one thousand times, and imagine ninja-fighting anyone who would dare try to harm your child.

On that day, something will wake up inside of your soul that can never go to sleep again. It's a little bit lion, a little bit lamb. A little bit ninja, and a little bit melted butter. It's a little bit "crying in the preschool parking lot" and a little bit "Thank goodness school is back in."

But, son, being a parent is the greatest gift God has ever given me, even on our hardest days. And I know, right now, you can't possibly know how that feels.

Not yet.

But one day (I hope), you will.

OUR

Picture

TAKE OUR PICTURE

On behalf of mamas everywhere, I have an important request:

Take our picture.

Even when we complain, even when our hair is a mess. Even when we are wearing a dingy, oversized sweatshirt.

Take our picture.

I know this isn't something on the forefront of your mind, and that's okay. We don't need every special moment documented, . . . but let's be honest.

We spend a lot of time doing just that for everyone else.

Please.

Take our picture.

Even when we fuss about how "chubby" we think we look in our swimsuit. If you see us splashing and laughing loudly with our babies in the heat of a gorgeous summer day—I don't care if we are nine months pregnant (*ahem*).

Take our picture.

Even if we moan that the angle isn't good or our smile looks a little insane, I promise you this: We want to be seen. We want to be remembered. And it means the world to us when you take our picture.

You may not realize it now, but we've taken hundreds of sneaky photos of you and the people you love.

When we see you snuggled on the couch with our babies or playing catch in the backyard, our hearts fill with joy and we can't help taking your picture.

Or maybe you DO realize it, and it's a little bit annoying. I can understand that, too.

> But here is a little reminder of why
> these pictures are SO dang important:

One day, we won't be around for our babies.

One day, you and I will be gone. What will remain of us will be the memories we've captured of this beautiful life we made.

One day, our kids will gather around a table and scroll through images of these precious, fleeting days.

They will cry and laugh and commiserate.

They will say, "Remember that vacation? Remember that day?"

And it will be so, so beautiful.

But if every single picture was taken by their mamas, guess who won't be in those memories?

The mother of your children deserves to be seen, documented, and remembered.

Not through posed family portraits or hundreds of selfies. But as who she was—who she is *now*—in those real, special life moments.

I know we complain, and we don't make it easy. Love us enough to do it anyway.

For our sake and for yours.

For the sake of our babies . . .

Take our picture.

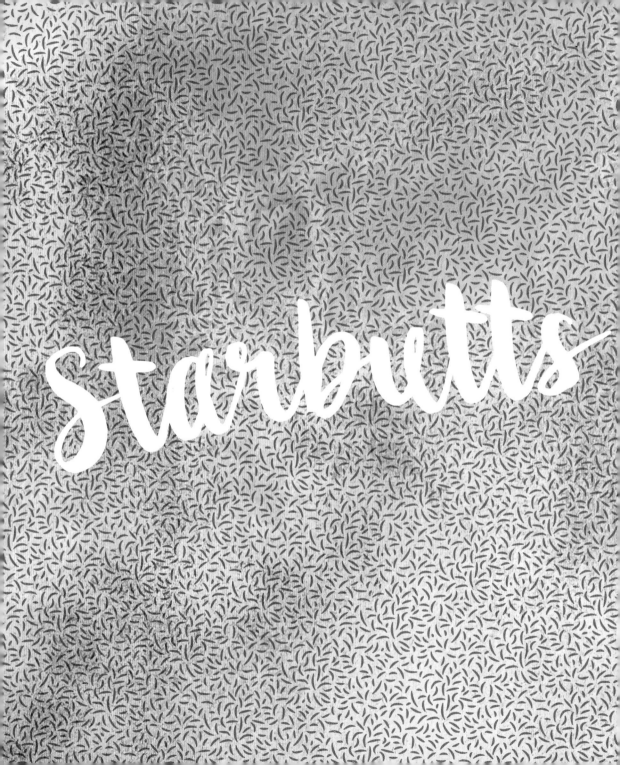

I Said

YES

I SAID YES

TODAY, MY LITTLE BOY ASKED ME TO HOLD HIM.

When he asked, of course, my hands were full. We had just gotten back from the grocery store, and it was ninety-eight degrees outside. My shirt was soaking wet from perspiration, and all I wanted was to get the heck inside. We live in South Florida, and there is no off-season for boob sweat here.

I wiped my forehead and looked down at Nugget, with his big hazel eyes.

"Mommy, please? Just carry me inside?"

It was so dang miserable that he had taken his shirt off in the car. I swear, even with AC blasting full throttle, his back was red and sticky from the heat.

Ben's skinny little arms reached out for me, like they've done nearly every day since he was a tiny babe. As if I could ever say no.

For a moment, though, I considered it.

The truth is, right now my back hurts. I've been sharing a bed with our two-year-old. She doesn't sleep well these days, between holiday travel and well, being a two-year-old.

I'm exhausted and perpetually sore.

But even so, I put down my bags and scooped my little boy out of his car seat.

Today, my little boy asked me to hold him.

And I said yes.

He is five years old right now. His legs dangle well past my waist, and the shape of his body doesn't lift as neatly as it did two years ago, when he was a toddler. By the time we made it to the back porch, I was huffing like an asthmatic buffalo. I struggled to put the key in the door and pushed it open with my foot. I let him down in the laundry room, and he slipped right through my arms and scampered away.

Maybe he was really tired. Maybe he wasn't. The truth is, my five-year-old probably could've walked inside from the car on his own.

I know the world may think he's too big, or that I'm babying him. But he's my son, and I'm his mama. And dang it, I have my own reasons. Don't mamas always have our reasons?

You see, every time his still-tiny voice asks me for something,

I wonder . . . Will this be the last time?

The last time I carry him inside from the car?

The last time he offers a butterfly kiss at bedtime?

The last time he asks for me to read just one more book?

The last time he draws a heart and a rainbow next to our stick figure family?

Of course I am aware my baby is getting big. His knobby knees and thinning cheeks remind me of that fact every, single day.

I am not oblivious to those judgmental gazes that find us in the grocery store parking lot as his head rests on my shoulder and his feet dangle well below my hips.

I see you, Doris. I know you disapprove.

But you know what else?

I know when my son holds my hand on the way into church, that those tiny little fingers won't be so generous with their grasp in the next few years.

I know when he crawls into my bed at three in the morning that his little spoon snuggles won't fit within my arms for many more seasons.

I know the years of needing and wanting his mommy in a public

and physical way are dwindling rapidly, right before my eyes.

So, excuse me for not caring what the whole world thinks. Let the Judgy McJudgersons and the Doris Downers whisper that my boy is "too big to be carried around like that."

I'm a mama, first and foremost, and my heart is already aching over how quickly these days are flying. If my back has to ache a little, too, what gives?

Because every mama knows that day is coming, all too soon. And then I'll be grateful for every single time that I said yes.

I AM not

The Mom

I
thought
I'D BE

I AM NOT THE MOM
I THOUGHT I'D BE

This is the thought I had yesterday as my child lay screaming on the floor because I wouldn't let him swish his fingers around in the toilet bowl (again). Tears streamed down his face—my betrayal had cut him to the core.

And there I sat, cross-legged on the closed toilet lid, laughing. Because, dang it, it was hilarious.

What else is a mama to do when it's 5:30 a.m., pre-caffeine, and the day's first meltdown is over toilet water?

As Nugget sent screamy-grams of suffering into the universe, I stood up to grab a towel and clean his hands.

And that is when a strange reflection in the mirror caught my eye.

Who . . . is . . . that?

There she was in all her glory. Her sleek braid casually strewn over one shoulder. A slight blush colored her cheeks. Her eyebrows were cleanly arched and a pressed shirt fell elegantly over her slender form.

And as she lifted one finger to wag in my face, a shiver went down my spine.

Oh, no! It's . . .

The Mother I Thought I'd Be!

I'd seen her before, most recently in the Wendy's drive-thru. I was ordering some fries to keep Ben occupied for a long drive. And as I adjusted the rearview mirror . . . there she was. Her perfect face staring back at me, mouth pursed in judgment.

"You should have ordered the apple slices," she hissed.

I froze in horror. I blinked a few times and rubbed my eyes.

"Ma'am . . . your fries." Friendly Wendy looked concerned as she tossed the bag through my car window. I pulled up twenty feet and promptly threw it in the trash. Like a crazy person.

Because, y'all . . . I am haunted.

Haunted by the ghosts of mommy insecurity.

I can't blame the Pinterest parents for my feelings. I can't blame my own mother (she's too supportive). I can't even blame those Stepford moms at the YMCA. (Full makeup at Boot Camp? Come on!)

No, my insanity is driven by the constant fear that I am falling short of the mom I wanted to be. That Nugget is getting royally ripped off.

That I should be doing much, much better.

You see, the Mother I Thought I'd Be (MITIB) would never be found laughing like a banshee on the john. She would have drawn some water in the sink and redirected Ben's toilet water game. She'd be splishy-splashing away, bubbles filling up the bathroom. Talking about things like water displacement because, you know, educational moments are everywhere!

Then, MITIB would have cleaned the bathroom floor with an "Oh, kids!" kind of giggle and moved on to the next enriching activity.

I strive to be her, but I can't keep up. She is so busy doing yoga and crafts and family pictures and Christmas cards. She's everything I wish to be, but if I'm being completely honest . . .

I hate her. We would never be friends.

I can't handle her sanctimonious lectures or her rigid schedule. Her food sucks. And I'm not even sure where my iron is! I throw my hubby's dress shirts in the dryer. (Shhh, don't tell!)

The Mother I Thought I'd Be? She's perfect. And I don't stand a chance of filling her patent leather heels.

But as I sit here watching my toddler roll around on the tiles, kicking his grief out in violent little lashes, I have to tell you . . .

He isn't the kid I thought he'd be, either.

So I scoop him off the bathroom floor and wipe his hands clean of toilet water. I look into those beautiful green eyes and giggle.

Yep. We both have some pretty rough edges.

But we fit together juuuuust right.

Enough

I know how ridiculous and selfish that is. He was two. I was THIRTY-two. And yet that feeling of resentment continued to rise up within me like acid after Mexican food.

So I football-carried Nugget all the way upstairs and unceremoniously dumped him, screaming, into his crib so I could tend to his sister.

Five minutes later he was still screaming. Ten minutes later, fifteen minutes later.

Twenty minutes later, I returned to his room, threw my hands in the air, and yelled again.

"What is wrong, Ben!"

His eyes widened. He clutched his blanket and whispered, "Mommy, I am scared."

My son was scared. Of me. Because I had raised my voice and lost my temper. Because my eyes probably revealed the anger inside my heart.

I spent the next thirty minutes in the rocking chair playing with his curly hair and singing his favorite songs. I whispered in his ear over and over again that I was sorry and that I loved him.

He eventually fell asleep.

I curled up on the couch, knowing he would wake up in an hour and ask for some apple juice and goldfish. He would be just fine.

But I was not fine.

I felt like a failure. I was utterly lost.

Who allowed me to have two kids? I wasn't ready for this. I was not qualified. Sure, I loved them with all my heart and I did my very best.

I would walk through fire for those little tots . . . but I was terrified I would screw things up. I was sure that's exactly what I was doing.

In my heart of hearts, I believed I was not good enough to do this job as a mother.

Let me tell you. In that moment of quiet despair, when I felt wrecked in my failure, God spoke to me in a still, small voice. One word was all I heard. It wasn't an audible voice, as much as a powerful whisper I could hear in my soul.

"Enough."

That was it. The word I needed to hear. Like a parent hushing a room, my Heavenly Father hushed the doubts raging inside of my heart.

"Enough."

Enough of the guilt.

Enough of the self-hatred and the shame.

Enough of the tears and worry and doubt.

Enough.

God made me to be the mother of these two beautiful children. I was not put in this position by mistake. Strong enough, resilient enough, to get through this season I am in.

Enough.

When life gets messy and we screw up at this parenting thing, there will be grace for us. There is grace enough for you and for me.

There is grace.

Enough to start over when naptime ends.

Every Day

I TELL MY

DAUGHTER

SHE IS

Beautiful

EVERY DAY I TELL MY
DAUGHTER SHE IS BEAUTIFUL

I COMPLIMENT HER BROWN EYES, HER BIG SMILE, AND HER WILD, UNTAMABLE HAIR. She twirls in her cheap, polyester gown and dances like a Disney princess. I can tell by the grin on her face she believes me.

And why wouldn't she? She's three.

I know some people believe it's unwise to praise a child's beauty, but I promise, I have my reasons. Hear me out.

You see, one day my daughter will go out into the world and hear a voice that isn't mine. Maybe it will be a boy in her class. Maybe it will be a girl. Maybe it will be a commercial or a billboard.

And that wicked voice will tell my beautiful child that she is less than. That she is falling short of a standard she didn't even know existed.

They'll tell her she's . . . unbeautiful.

Every woman alive knows this feeling. We either believed it was true for a time, or we still struggle to unbelieve it now.

How much would we give to spare
our own daughters this heartache?

I'd give just about anything.

Lord, how I cling to these easy days, when Holland's childlike innocence protects her. It makes my heart sing that she can put on a two-dollar plastic tiara and believe she's actual royalty.

She's a *beautiful* little human, and right now she knows it.

Because, you see, I have told her a million times.

When she builds a tower with her Legos, I tell her that intelligence is *beautiful*.

When she climbs the ladder at the playground, and falls, then dusts herself off to try again, I tell her that determination is *beautiful*.

When she paints with her fingers, a pink little pig with lopsided eyes and a clown-like smile, I tell her that creativity is *beautiful*.

When she introduces herself to a quiet kid on the playground, I tell her that kindness is *beautiful*.

When she chases our puppy around the backyard until her curly hair is matted to her sweaty forehead, I tell her that strength and exercise are *beautiful*.

One day, some voice will whisper lies to my daughter. Maybe they'll mock her eyes or her smile, or her thighs or her clothes or her nose. They will tell my child, my perfect little girl . . .

That she isn't beautiful.

But my hope is this:

That my daughter will blink away her tears and remember that beauty isn't the shape of the body God gave her. That beauty isn't the form of a face.

No, she'll remember what we've told her a million times: that beauty is everything she's made of and all of who she is.

That she can grow old, or lose her hair, or be overweight or dress like the pits of fashion—

And always, always be beautiful.

YOUR

Mother

CALL YOUR MOTHER

I walked in to get my hair cut, and a small Persian woman introduced herself. My former stylist had moved back home, she explained. Her name was Nina, and she was taking over Michelle's client list.

I quickly liked Nina. She had a quiet beauty about her. She asked me what I did, and I explained that I was a mother who enjoyed writing. I talked about Mom Babble, and her interest piqued.

"It is a mother's blog?"

"Yes, that's what people call it."

"I wish to tell you about my mother."

So she did. She told me about a woman whose laughter makes men stop in the grocery store. Who sleeps with her hand balled up by her mouth. She walks like a ballerina and keeps secrets, and smells like comfort food. She never judges, and is soft and lovely. She has a strong faith.

"My mother is my best friend," she said.

I asked if she would get to see her mom for Thanksgiving. She paused, setting down the scissors.

"My mother passed seventeen years ago. But it feels like yesterday."

Sadness filled her brown eyes. Nina shook her head as if to get rid of a thought, then picked up her scissors. She continued clipping in silence, and I realized she was trying desperately to maintain her composure. After a few moments, she drew a breath.

"I no longer celebrate this holiday. It only reminds me that my childhood is gone. It is gone, along with my mother."

And then I understood.

Because I had just returned from a weekend with my best friend. We have the same laugh. The same ski slope nose and black hair. She cooks me Southern food, takes me for pedicures, and we drink sugary lattes together.

And when I'm with her, I feel like a child.

Our relationship has the depth and width of my entire life. She was there for burp cloths and Easter baskets, stitches and puberty. Boyfriends and college plans and wedding dress shopping. She was at bedside for the delivery of my son. My mother isn't just my best friend. She's the vessel that holds my childhood.

Edna St. Vincent Millay once wrote, "Childhood is the kingdom where nobody dies."

Perhaps that is true . . . or partially so. You see, that kingdom exists within our parents. And when they are gone, our childhoods become a memory. A story we tell our own children as they yawn and wiggle in their car seats. A book stacked neatly on a shelf is treasured for the story it contains. To be read, told, and treasured, but never lived again.

I wanted so desperately to get out of that salon chair and call my mama. Instead, I sat in the heavy silence that marked the end of our transaction. I watched as Nina pulled my black locks straight. There was so much to say, but I couldn't find the words. So I ran my fingers through my freshly cut mane and smiled.

"It's a fantastic haircut. I love it."

Nina smiled, handing me a mirror, so I could inspect the final product. She spun the chair left and right, until I placed the mirror in my lap and said thank you. Then she walked me to check-out where, for once, I happily paid salon price.

I wanted to hug this woman, but she didn't give me the hugging vibe. I wanted to tell her thank-you, but the truth was those words—like the generous tip I scribbled on the receipt at checkout—would feel insufficient.

So I left with a wave and heart heavy with gratitude. Nina was already greeting her next client by the time I walked out of the door. No doubt, her business was going to be successful.

She was really good at cutting hair.

I got in my car, snapped the seat belt, and took a selfie of my fresh new "do." I added the picture to a text message, and scrolled down to the M's in my contacts to select a recipient: Mom.

I paused for a moment, then deleted the message. I hit the button that beckons Siri and spoke with a shaky voice: "Call mom."

It only took two rings for a familiar voice to answer.

"Hello?"

"Hey, Mom?" My voice cracked again, and I was a little embarrassed that it was giving me away.

"I was just calling to say I love you."

SOMETHING

Stinks

SOMETHING STINKS

SOMETIMES I FEEL LIKE I'VE GOT THIS PARENTING THING UNDER CONTROL.

And other times my three-year-old daughter sets her basket down, pulls off her heirloom smocked pantaloons, and pees like a racehorse during the family's annual Easter egg hunt.

What I've learned is that whether my children decide to act like hellions or angels on any given day has very little to do with me, the way I discipline, or the amount of Jesus we have in our household.

How do I know this?

Because I'm the same mama all day, every day, but which kid I get on a daily basis is just about as reliable as the weather.

Will I get a Shirley Temple daughter who sings like a cherub and pats my face and tells me with her baby voice that she "lubs me more dan cupcakes"?

Or will I get the holy terror who tells the deacon at church: "When

I get home imma rip this dress off so I can be nekkid and SCREAM like a bear. RAAAAWR!"

Who knows? It's a coin toss.

Will I get the son who smiles with his eyes and uses "yes, ma'am" and "thank you, sir" and holds my hand in the parking lot like a commercial for joining Boy Scouts?

Or will I get the unpredictable over-sharer who informed his preschool teacher that sometimes he can't sleep at night because his mama told him serial killers grab children from their beds?

(I never said that. *Ever. Evaaar.*)

Luck of the draw, folks. I literally never know which kid will show up. I just bring the circus and hold my breath.

It's a lottery, I guess.

But then, if you have more than one child, the statistics get a bit more complicated. Some days one kid is great and the other kid is a nightmare. That's manageable.

Some days the math works in your favor, God smiles down upon you, and both children are PBS cartoon angels.

But, oh.

Oooohhhhhh, some days.

Some days you'll be dragging one child by the foot through the grocery store while yelling at the other kid, *"If you open that can of Pringles I will throw your puppy in the trash can!"* (Not realizing that the entire store thinks the puppy is a flesh-and-blood creature of God, as opposed to the piece of one-inch-tall plastic crap that it is.)

Some days we lose big.

And of course, some days we win.

All I'm saying, parents, is if you are having a winning streak, don't you dare get cocky.

Don't. You. Dare.

Your kiddos will knock you off that high horse quicker than you can say "dead bird snuck to school in a backpack."

And if you're on a losing streak, parents, listen to me.

Listen. To. Me.

Today I found out that my daughter sneaks into a room in our house, puts on a pull-up, poops in it, throws the poop in an actual garbage can, and puts her panties back on like nothing ever happened.

Tomorrow, I get to apologize to our cleaning ladies for the fact they've been cleaning *human waste* out of a trash can on a weekly basis.

And now I am dealing with the shame and confusion over why the ladies never mentioned this to me. Like, is this just what they accept from

STAY HUMBLE, AND CHECK YOUR TRASH CANS.

the Backstrom family? The bar is so low when they come into our household that this is a norm they have come to accept and ignore?

Poop in trash cans?

You might be having a rough week, Mama, but here's some encouragement: it could probably be worse.

You might be having a great week, but here's a bit of warning: it could turn quickly.

All I am saying is that no matter how hard you try as a parent, and no matter how perfect your kids are behaving today . . . you never know where the next mystery trash-can turd will show up in your life.

So I guess the moral of this story is to stay humble, my friends.

Stay humble, and check your trash cans.

YOUR

Number?

WHAT'S YOUR NUMBER?

185.

That's my number.

It is what pops up on the scale when I'm in the doctor's office. Or when I step out of the shower and dry my hair and use the bathroom and decide that it's time to torture myself over three little figures.

One. Eight. Five.

sigh

Or is it 14?

Maybe that's my number.

I gained ten pounds and two sizes with each new baby. Calling it baby weight is a bit of a stretch at this point. It's been half a decade. This is who I am now.

Or is it 390?

Maybe that's my number.

The size implant I think I want when they reconstruct my post-mastectomy breasts so I can feel a little more human again.

I squeezed every weird gelatin blob in my plastic surgeon's office before settling on one that, quite honestly, looked like all the others.

"I dunno, this one?"

The nurse jotted down some numbers, looked over my body, and left the room.

It was a bizarre place to be, sitting in an open gown, with my marshmallow tummy and stitched up breasts exposed.

Even more bizarre was sitting next to a wall covered with plastic surgery pamphlets. Each featured a woman who was smiling in a crisp linen shirt and, I assume, was so very happy because she had some sort of voluntary surgical procedure. I was there because of cancer. It wasn't exactly voluntary.

But my curiosity was piqued.

I grabbed a few brochures and thumbed through them: brow lifts, arm lifts, tummy tucks, lipo, Botox, Mommy makeovers, eyelid lifts . . .

Did you know that your face has "parentheses" on it? Apparently, they aren't desirable.

I always thought they were smile lines, but according to the brochures you can fill them in with medical jelly stuff and make them go away.

And then it's like you never smiled at all!

Which is . . . good, I guess?

With all that reading material, it was hard not to imagine what my body would look like if I had a smaller waist. Or bigger boobs. Fewer wrinkles. Rounder butt. Smoother legs. Flab-free arms.

I hadn't considered these things before . . . but they seemed like really good ideas.

When the nurse returned, I put my clothes back on, paid my co-pay, and returned home.

I stood in front of the mirror and just stared at my body.

I never realized my arms jiggled when I waved. Maybe an arm lift would fix that.

I never realized I had parentheses on my face. Goodness, can you actually smile too much?

I never considered that the veins showing under my skin were unsightly. My kids always traced their tiny fingers over them like it was a game. I kinda liked that game until just now.

My mind raced.

What was it Sir Mix-a-Lot said?

"36-24-36. Hah, only if she's 5'3!"

Thank goodness it occurred to me that I shouldn't care what Sir Mix-a-Lot thinks about a woman's body.

I'm ashamed to say that it took a bit longer for me to realize that he isn't the only one whose opinion I shouldn't care about.

Y'all still with me?

Good. Because I need to tell you something.

Those numbers? Those ideals? Those crazy standards we are literally starving ourselves and cutting ourselves open to comply with?

They are all lies.

I am serious.

Who came up with a "parentheses" anyways? These are smile lines.

I smile because I am happy.

The world can deal with it.

This insanity that has gripped our society is so toxic that we are all ashamed of our weight, our size, and our age. We spend half our lives trying to fix ourselves with diet, exercise, and surgery, like those things have any bearing at all on who misses us when we are gone.

Listen to me.

There is no formula that makes you beautiful.

My numbers will never add up to society's ideal.

I am pale, I've had multiple surgeries, and I weigh 185 pounds.

I'm a size 14. I'm 35 years old.

Do you think those are the numbers that define me?

Or is it possible they literally. Mean. Nothing?

I am here to tell you that this world has bumped its head. Society is paying attention to all the wrong things.

There are no stats on the planet that could convey your worth. There are too many undefined variables. It's crap math, and it doesn't add up.

My pants size can't tell you that I've brought two children into this world. Wanna know that number?

Two.

Pretty awesome if you ask me.

My age doesn't tell you about my thirteen years of marriage. Thirteen. That's a number I'm pretty dang proud of.

My figure stats don't reveal that I donated a kidney, or recently underwent a mastectomy. My bra size doesn't tell anyone I'm a breast cancer survivor.

Because, *hello*. Those numbers do not matter.

They never did.

Friends, I hope you never again look in the mirror and cry over curves and wrinkles.

I hope you never look at the scale and believe the lie that it somehow defines you.

When society's ideal numbers crowd your brain and break your spirit and make you question your worth, I want you to remember your good ole friend, MK.

I am here, enjoying my life—with crow's-feet and frankenboobs, smile lines, and cottage cheese thighs.

One hundred eighty-five pounds. Size 14. Thirty-five years old.

And none of it matters a bit.

You and I are creations whose value cannot be defined. We are loved by God and we are perfect the way we are.

Yes. I said it: *perfect*.

Our worth is innate.

It is *infinite*, my friends.

And infinity is a number that simply can't be counted.

"I MADE

You

FROM
Scratch,
YOU KNOW."

"I MADE YOU FROM SCRATCH, YOU KNOW."

MAMA USED TO SAY THAT ALL THE TIME WHEN I WAS YOUNG. And she always seemed to say it when I tried to do something fun. It was a statement that often followed "be careful" or "no, you can't do that," so I got tired of hearing it. I would roll my eyes when she said it.

Like, "Geez, I get it, lady. You gave birth to me. Now let me do my thing!"

I fell from tree branches. I tore up my knees Rollerblading in the street. I busted my lip playing backyard football with the boys. I tied wagons to the backs of bicycles with jump ropes and took my cousins for "sleigh rides" around the neighborhood streets.

And no matter how many times she cautioned me to be careful, and no matter how many times I threw that caution to the wind . . . my mama would be there with an ice pack, a hug, and a reminder that:

"I made you from scratch, you know."

Years later, my son burst into this world with the wimpiest cry my nurse had ever heard. As I was laid out on that hospital bed, exhausted and unable to move, I watched with panic as my sister grabbed the suction bulb and saved my little baby's developing brain. It was just a little aspiration, he would be fine.

The literal first seconds of my child's life, I held him to my chest with my heart racing and a strange, unfamiliar mixture of emotions rushed over me—what was it?

Anger? Fear? Relief?

All of it.

He's five now, with a three-year-old sister.

It probably doesn't have to be said but these kids don't give a rip about the world of danger around them.

They play with reckless abandon on playground equipment that I swear towers so high it practically touches the clouds.

"Be careful!" I yell, like the neurotic helicopter mom I never thought I'd be.

Don't these kids know I made them from scratch?

Babes don't come from some cake box recipe. They are—every

single part—handcrafted and unique, put together with love and intention.

You can't replace them, and there isn't a mama on the planet who would ever dare to try. The idea is unfathomable. There's no one like them in this world, and there never will be again.

As every good cook knows, there's always a little love thrown in the mix when you are making something from scratch. In the moment, you just know the recipe calls for a little something extra. Something that wouldn't work any other day of the week, but on this special occasion, will make the batch complete.

It's not written on paper, and there's no record of its existence. But the cook who made the batch from scratch, knows exactly what's in it.

Every good cook knows.

And so does every mom.

When my daughter came running up to me last week with her first bloody knee, I nearly cried. But I composed myself so her eyes wouldn't know my fear.

I kissed her boo-boo and made an ice pack. I smelled her sweet curls that still have just a hint of babiness in them. Then I pulled her in for a hug and whispered, "Be careful, baby. I made you from scratch, you know."

She toddled back toward the playground that touches the clouds, and I knew in my heart why my mom had bugged me all those years . . .

We throw our entire hearts into the mix with our children, and it's with them wherever they go.

They are made from scratch, you know.

SOME

Children

ARE JUST

Born Feral

SOME CHILDREN ARE
JUST BORN FERAL

PARENTS CAN POTTY TRAIN, SLEEP TRAIN, AND TEACH MANNERS until their brains are about to explode, but some children, who for some reason God only knows, can't be tamed.

They are the kids who pull their diapers off and swing them around their heads like lassos. Yeehaw, Mr. Mailman! OMG, sorry, I didn't realize the door was open.

They are the kids who eat dead bugs off the floor and shove TNT snap-n-pops into their ear canals.

They are the kids who meet your emergency room deductible by February.

They are the kids who are responsible for your forehead wrinkles and every, single gray hair.

They play too close to the water, run through the hallways with forks while eating grapes, and somehow (like really, HOW?) climb the fireplace mantel.

So what should parents do with these tiny little wildebeests?

Society certainly has opinions. Experts have their theories. Authors have their books. Pharmacies have their pharms.

Little old ladies are gonna stop and shake their heads and their long, wrinkled fingers, because they think they know.

But, parents, listen to me right now because I'm gonna save you some serious heartache and stress:

Nothing is gonna tame a feral-born child!

So cover your electric outlets with plastic plugs and anchor your furniture to the floor. Hide your batteries on the highest shelf and lower that crib mattress a little more.

Hide your pets, put your forks and knives in a secret drawer. (Then maybe move them once a week, just to be safe.)

Because you aren't going to tame that feral child. Best you can hope for is to simply survive them.

And if some Know-It-All wants to tell you otherwise, you go find them a drunk and hungry hyena. Shove it into some Doc McStuffins Pull-ups, and drop it off at that Know-It-All's house.

Tell him it likes to eat broccoli and really needs a bath.

Then go back in twenty-four hours and see how confident Mr. Know-It-All still feels about parenting your feral-born child.

Now it's true that parents of feral children are tired. Our hair is all frazzled and our houses are falling apart brick by brick. We've given up patching the dry wall. We are just gonna get it done with a multiple hole Groupon discount when we move out. (Is that a thing? It should be a thing.)

The truth is, we have long since given up on trying to impress the world with our awesome parenting skills.

We are okay with the fact that our child is wild.

We are okay with the mess and the noise.

Believe it or not, we even *relish it.*

(A little bit.)

Because only a feral child can teach you to see the world through an unfiltered lens. Only a feral child can see a world of adventure in a 1/8 acre flat, grassy lawn. Only a wild, unadulterated spirit knows the joy of streaking through the house after a bath, screaming like a banshee and feeling the wind on their buck-naked skin.

It's a little crazy, but let's be honest: it's pretty freaking fun.

Some children are just born feral. It's true.

The sooner we accept that, the better off we will be. And just a thought, but maybe . . . just maybe . . .

We have a little bit to learn from these wild-at-heart, freedom-filled, life-relishing little humans.

I dreamed of being
SOMETHING
Great

...now I'm a

Mother

I DREAMED OF BEING
SOMETHING GREAT. . .
NOW I'M A MOTHER

2002. YEAR OF SPAGHETTI STRAP TANK TOPS, flavored lip gloss, and one-dollar gasoline. Diet Coke added lime to their cans. Michael Jackson dangled a baby over a balcony, and Nickleback ruled *Billboard* charts.

So, yeah—a few regrettables, but altogether, it was a pretty good year. I was a senior in high school. And graduation was around the corner. Our school newspaper published the Senior Edition, a tongue-in-cheek prequel to the yearbook. The graduating class voted Who's Who in silly categories and anonymously submitted thoughts and jokes for a segment titled "In Ten Years I See."

The day that newspaper came out I was probably rocking flare-cut Mudd jeans and a homecoming T-shirt, eating my daily breakfast of a Fudge Round and Diet Mountain Dew. (How was I so skinny? Lord only knows.)

The papers hit the stands after first period and students devoured the material with nostalgic smiles. I opened the paper and ran my finger down the page, searching for the segment I was most excited to read. I spotted my name a few rows from the top.

In ten years I see . . .

Mary Katherine Samples having great ideas and never following through.

To say the wind was taken out of my sails would be an understatement. More like somebody ripped the sails off my happy little boat and used them as toilet paper. I read that line over and over again, chewing on it until all the flavor was gone. I tried to find a version of that joke funny or flattering. It wasn't.

Chances are I was the only person who read that one-liner and kept thinking about it. But during the final weeks of school, I walked the halls of Northview High with raw feelings and a shattered ego. The sour reality was this: one of my classmates had met me, sized me up, and considered me a joke. And because my legacy was so laughable in their minds, so, apparently would be my future.

And that was worth immortalizing in the school paper.

Years later I was on a *Criminal Minds* marathon and decided to become an FBI agent. I changed my major to criminal psychology and

WHAT WILL MY LEGACY
BE TO THIS CHILD?

joined a hardcore gym. I jogged five miles a day, wore ponytails, and used terms like "MO" and "perp."

Unfortunately, after all that "training," my FBI dream died. This was due to the fact that, apparently, I was prone to shin splints. Also, I didn't look cute in a baseball cap. You may not know this, but it's very important that you can wear the FBI baseball cap if you are going to be a serious FBI agent. So, that dream was dead before it really took off. But, nevermind all that—my (new) true passion was to own and train a wild American Mustang. So, naturally, I went out and bought one. His name was Trigger, and it's a miracle I'm still alive.

In the last decade or so I've dreamed of becoming an FBI agent, author, astronaut, rock star, horse trainer, and food-truck owner. And as of this moment, I am finally one of those things. But it took years, y'all. Twenty of them.

♥

And long before my book deal ever came to fruition, I found myself rocking my infant son to sleep. He was sweet against my chest, purring like a tiny little train. I was drifting off to sleep myself, when a *Criminal Minds* rerun came on the television. I laughed softly, recalling the absurdity of my FBI dream. It was a pleasant, silly memory at first. But then, from some dark rafter within my mind, a voice whispered, "In ten years I see . . ."

A pit was forming in my stomach as I lay Ben down in his crib. I stared at my son, fighting off tears, and wondered, what will my legacy be to this child?

His mom: the never-gonna-happen FBI agent? His mom: the unpublished author? The half-baked rock star who almost got on TV?

Depressing.

I curled up on the couch with a cup of coffee, flipping through channels and wondering what I had to show for myself these last ten years. The thought wasn't an inspiring one. I was pretty far into a state of self-pity when the sound of a waking baby saved me.

As I retrieved Ben from his crib, he smiled and planted an open-mouthed kiss on my cheek. He cooed, "Mama! Mama!" from his perch on my hip. I set him down on the playroom floor.

It was in that hour, when I needed it most, that my son took his very first steps. He came crashing into my arms with a toothy grin and a joyous giggle. And then I realized.

My legacy.

A green-eyed boy who is not yet afraid of falling. Who is discovering his world with confidence because his home—the home I make every day—is safe and secure.

My legacy.

A son who will know there is strength in tears. Who will adore his father. Who will understand what it is to wrestle with faith–but never lose it.

My legacy.

A boy who will memorize *Goodnight Moon* because it was read to him a thousand times. Who will always know the safety net of his mother's hug.

And now, when I think about it, in ten years I see:

Mary Katherine Backstrom mending boo-boos. Conquering the boogie man. Comforting heartaches. Laughing at knock-knock jokes. Cooking pancakes, throwing baseballs, and mopping muddy floors. Relishing in the beautiful, constant noise that is a life with children.

And if this child be the sole legacy I leave in this world . . .

I can be pretty dang proud of my life.

It's easy to forget this lesson, sometimes. It's one I have to constantly "reteach" myself, even as I'm preaching it to my friends and fellow parents. But it's a truth of biblical proportions, isn't it? Moths, rust, and thieves can steal away our trophies and accumulated treasures in this world. But the tiny souls we've been given stewardship over?

Those are *eternal*.

What an incredible gift and legacy we have in our children.

Is there any higher calling on this earth than that of a parent?

I haven't been a mother very long, . . . but I have a sneaking suspicion this is the greatest job on the entire planet.

OUT OF THE

Mouths

Of
Babes

OUT OF THE MOUTHS OF BABES

I HAD ALREADY HAD A LONG DAY when it was time to put my daughter to bed. There had been deadlines and bills, marital arguments and financial stresses. I felt tired and physically worn.

All of that to say, I wasn't prepared for a knock-down, drag-out bedtime hour with my three-year-old.

But that is exactly what I got.

For an hour and a half, we were the Clash of the Titans. She wanted a water, and I refused.

"You'll have to pee in an hour."

"No, I'll *not*!"

She wanted apple juice, and I said no because she'd have to brush her teeth.

"You'll get sugar bugs, and they'll eat holes in your teeth!"

"I *like* holes in my teeth!"

Then she cried because her toothbrush didn't vibrate like her brother's.

"I want the toofbrush that goes *buzzbuzz*!"

"You wanted the Elsa toothbrush! Now go to sleep!"

She wanted a doll, but not that doll.

She wanted a pillow, but not that pillow.

An hour after this battle began, I finally quit fighting. I left her wriggling around the bed, walked away, and through clinched teeth, Batman voiced, "I love you, Holland, but I don't want to hear another word tonight. Not. Another. Word. You are going to sleep. We are done fussing over stuffed animals and juice and toothbrushes. Good NIGHT!"

"Mommy?"

I paused in the doorway, literally biting my tongue.

How does a tiny human have the ability to make me so crazy mad?

"What is it, Holland?"

"I DO have one more thing to say."

Of course she did. And with style. Holland stood on the bed, power stance and all. Hands on hips, her hair was wild. She used her arm to wipe tears and snot away from her face.

"Mommy," she said, staring me down with the slightest bit of venom in her voice . . .

"I FORGIVE YOU!"

Then she threw herself down, prostrate across the bed, and honest to goodness, for a hot minute, I didn't know what to do.

The way she'd said "I forgive you" made it sound like a bunch of cuss words. Was she mad? Was she sorry?

Was this some sort of Jedi mind trick?

I walked over to my daughter's bedside and leaned over.

Her shoulders shook and her little nose sniffled. Her face was shoved deep into her Little Mermaid pillow.

I felt my heart soften.

"Baby girl," I asked, "do you know what forgiveness means?"

"Yes," she muttered.

I really had to hear this.

"It means you were wrong, and I'm tired of being mad. Now I'm going to sleep, and my heart won't have a tummy ache."

Oof.

My stomach sank, and I was pretty sure I immediately knew what she meant by "her heart having a tummy ache."

I felt it, too.

I wanted nothing more than to relieve that sickness and be at peace with my precious child.

To be honest, that night I was taught a lesson in forgiveness by my three-year-old. It was a gut punch, too. I realized that even though my daughter spent the entire night pressing every button her mama had, it wasn't personal. My daughter wasn't *giving* me a hard time. She was *having* a hard time.

And the adult in the room had forgotten how to behave like one.

You better believe I crawled straight into her bed and held her tight until the tears and sadness subsided for both of us.

Because to be honest, *my* heart had a bit of a tummy ache, too. Turns out, a little grace was just the medicine both of us needed.

Sometimes, God uses the mouths of babes to remind us of his most important truths. This year, I was reminded by a toddler to never go to bed in anger.

According to Holland, when you go to bed angry, your heart ends up with a tummy ache. I've been alive for thirty-five years, and I've got to give it to the little girl:

She isn't wrong.

Grace

Chips

GRACE CHIPS

IT WAS AN HOUR PAST NAP TIME, but the Salty Dog Cafe was still on my husband's to-do list. Since I love him, or perhaps because I'm completely bonkers, we decided to brave the storm.

We carried two hangry children into the restaurant. When the server arrived to take our drink order, we were all, "Two Diet Cokes, an apple juice, a grilled cheese, some fish nuggets—oh, and do you have some crackers?"

Parents know the struggle.

We were in the corner of the restaurant, and the baby stopped crying JUST long enough to slam down a few oyster crackers. She was in my lap, and I maneuvered my hands around her body, while I inhaled a sandwich.

I started to resent my husband for entertaining this horrible idea. I'd voted for sandwiches at the condo. At least there, I could chew. Then Nugget decided to keep getting out of his chair "to go see the water," and frankly I was about to pull a "Jesus at the Temple-market" and send some tables flying.

My husband took the baby, handed Ben the fish basket, and said, "Hey, son. Why don't you have a picnic by the window?"

I must've looked at him like he was growing horns.

Great idea, hon. Let him eat on the filthy restaurant floor!

But I was desperate and on the brink, so that's exactly what my son ended up doing. In seconds, both kids were happy and the meal that started off like a trip through a broken car wash started to feel like a memory in the making.

Conversation changed to, "Remember how we were here just eleven years ago on our honeymoon?"

Stress turned to laughter. I began to actually chew. And chaos suddenly became a special memory.

I would like to say we handled this parenting crisis with ingenuity and skill, but, y'all, it was something a little less impressive:

We dropped the bar.

Yes, I said it: parents, sometimes we just have to *lower our standards.*

Tiny people aren't meant to regulate their emotions, hunger, boredom, and exhaustion the same way adults do. They just can't. And

Parents, sometimes we just have to lower our standards.

unless you want to be a hermit for the next five years, you're gonna have to accept that imperfection happens.

If a picnic on a dirty floor buys you a moment's peace, I say go for it. If the baby is drinking tiny sips of Daddy's Sprite, and it keeps her from melting down, well a quarter cup of soda never killed anybody.

Overlooking the water, Nugget chewed on a French fry. A woman at the table behind us turned around in her seat. She was definitely preparing to make some commentary, and my stomach dropped a little.

"His curls are so adorable." She smiled at me. "My son right here used to have the same exact hair!"

Her teenage son laughed and waved, and in that moment, I relished in the beauty that is this sisterhood of moms.

We all have a certain amount of grace chips when we get started, don't we?

My husband handed me a grace chip when he took the baby. That mom handed me a grace chip when she completely ignored our floor picnic and instead complimented my kid.

And today, I want to hand a grace chip to all of you, in hopes that you might pay it forward.

Parenting is hard. Sometimes we just have to

drop the bar in order to get over it.

None of us are perfect. We all require grace—and folks, that's okay.

Because luckily, we all have some grace to give.

Take a moment to jingle those grace chips in your pocket, and remember this, moving forward:

You have the power to impact somebody else's life today. All you have to do is reach into your pocket and pull out a grace chip. Share a smile with the family whose kid is eating fish nuggets on the floor of the Salty Dog. Give that stressed out mama a reprieve from public shame.

Don't be stingy with grace chips, friends. The things you pass around in this world tend to come back around to you. When you see someone else struggling and it's your turn to dig into your pocket and dish a little something out . . . remember this:

Make it kindness. Make it grace.

Letting

Go

LETTING GO

I'M A PARENT.

My time is not my own. My body is not my own. My bed is not my own.

My shower is not my own. My food is not my own. My personal space . . . nope.

I couldn't have prepared for this. Motherhood came crashing down on me the moment my son entered the world. Where I had a tight grip on things I thought were *mine*, motherhood loosened my fingers.

Slowly, bit by bit, I lost sovereignty over my schedule. My privacy. Even at times, my body (hello, breast pump).

But after motherhood pulled each finger away from the things I clung to, after my hand was spread open and empty . . .

Well, I got the privilege of having

fat little fingers intertwined in mine.

So, ask me if I'd do it all again. If I'd trade away my freedom, my figure, the luxury of peeing alone . . .

Ask me what I'd be willing to give to live this life where *nothing* is my own.

I'll tell you right now, the answer is . . .

Everything.

Claim

BAGGAGE CLAIM

AFTER A ZILLION HOURS OF TRAVEL DISASTERS, I ended up sitting by the baggage claim in the Atlanta airport with a two-year-old Nugget in my lap. Except my son wasn't really himself. He was being a hangry-toddler-demon-monster version of himself.

As I pinned his arms to his side, he thrashed his little body around like a beached shark and screamed little toddler screams into the universe.

And I just sat still watching the luggage spin. Hair frazzled. Overwhelmed.

And even though every cell in my body fought against the onslaught of tears, they came in ugly, silent sobs.

I was so tired, embarrassed, and frustrated. I had a headache and was just *done*.

But motherhood wasn't done with me. Bedtime was a rental car and thirty miles away.

And as I sat there crying with a tiny, angry shark in my lap, the strangest thing happened.

This sweet mama walked by with her posse of kids in tow. She gave me the sign of the cross, winked, and smiled. As she rolled her suitcase toward the spinning glass doors, she spoke one single word to me:

"Sisterhood."

And oh my tears just poured. But now they flowed for an entirely different reason.

I no longer felt alone in a weary battle. I was reminded that I had comrades. People who understand me, who didn't judge me, and who loved me all the same.

Isn't it incredible how easy it is to touch another life? How simple it is to make a gesture that gives somebody the strength they need to carry on?

All it takes is a smile and a word of kindness to reach someone just where they are and pull them out of a valley. And in case you need a reminder, the world today is full of folks who have been where you are, know how you feel, and are whispering "sisterhood" to you through these pages.

You aren't alone in your struggles. Motherhood is the great equalizer. I don't care who you are, at some point every three-year-old on the planet has a "tiny shark in the airport baggage claim" moment.

The only question is, will you be crying on the bench, or will you be the mama walking by?

Do me a favor, please. If you are lucky enough to be the mama walking by, can you throw that crying mama a smile? A line of solidarity or a friendly wink?

Something as simple as a tiny "you've got this" can truly change everything for a mother who is at the end of her rope and slipping.

It did for me. It made a world of difference.

That mama reminded me that my crazy, hectic, nightmare-of-an-evening was just a little bit funny. She reminded me that I wasn't alone and that I would get through this. In that one second of solidarity, I was able to fast-forward my brain to a moment in time where I was her, breezing through the airport with older, gentler children. That was all I needed.

I wiped my tears, football-carried my child to the rental car, and made it all the way home.

All of that from the power of one single word: *sisterhood.*

I don't want to imagine how that could've gone differently. How my heart could've been further crushed by a judgy comment or a hateful glare. All I know is I was spared the hurt and given the grace I so desperately needed.

Mamas. Listen to me.

There is a whole world of sisters out there in need of encouragement, and one word—*one single word*—can change their days, maybe even their lives, for the better.

Knowing you have that superpower, don't you want to get up and go do something with it? Get out there today. Take a word of kindness and solidarity out into the wild. Find a mama who has a shark in her lap and let her know she is loved.

Mary

Poppins

MARY POPPINS

I'M NOT A PERFECT MAMA. I AM DOING THE BEST I CAN. Sometimes my best looks a lot like Kraft Mac & Cheese and boxed apple juice. Or Mickey Mouse and pajamas till dinner time.

But on other days my best looks like pancakes in the morning and strolls to the park. Or tree-climbing and puddle-splashing till sundown.

On a good day, I put Mary Poppins to shame.

Two different days, I might be two different mamas. Nugget never knows who he's gonna wake up to.

But you know what's freaking awesome? He doesn't care. Every night as I leave his room, I crack open the door and whisper:

"Hey Nugget, who loves you the most in the entire world?"

And regardless of whether we had a crackers-for-dinner day or a puddle-jumping, Mary Poppins day, his response is always the same:

"My mama."

WHO LOVES YOU THE MOST
IN THE ENTIRE WORLD?

THE
Day

I WAS

Left

Behind

THE DAY I WAS LEFT BEHIND

I WOKE UP THIS MORNING TO A VERY STRANGE SENSATION. Something was off, but I couldn't quite put my finger on it. I grabbed my phone to check the time.

8:00 a.m.!

Strange sensation, indeed! I am *rested*. How was this possible? Was I still asleep?

I scrambled for the baby monitor: offline. My heart started racing. The room was so . . . so . . . *silent*!

Where was my snoring husband?

I rushed to the bathroom to put in my contacts. When my blindness subsided, I was not prepared for what I saw.

Clothes, melted over themselves, in a pile of absent humanness.

Oh. My. Lord. I've been *left behind*!

The dogs were barking next door. I bet my neighbors had been zapped up, too. Great. Just, great. It's just me . . . and . . . the *babies*?

I rushed to the kitchen, and my worst fears were affirmed.

The creamer was out. The fridge was open. Coffee cups, remnants of breakfast, toppled sippy cups. All evidence of a family that no longer resided in my home.

This can't be happening. This can't be happening.

I walked like a zombie into the den. A Netflix movie streamed on the TV. No husband. No babies.

My palms were sweating when I reached for my cell phone. A part of me hoped for a baby to appear and be here with me, but the other part . . . I couldn't bear to consider it.

I typed in my pass code.

My screen loaded slowly.

There was a voice message. I held my breath and held the phone to my ear.

"Good morning, honey. At the park. Kids and I thought you could use the rest."

I sat on the couch and sighed in relief. I knew it was absurd, running around the house searching for ghosts of the rapture. But knowing something is ridiculous and stopping yourself from feeling it are entirely different. I leaned back into the pillow and willed my heart rate to slow down.

Count your blessings, MK. Count your blessings.

Blessing one. My family wasn't sucked up into heaven without me. Thank you, Jesus.

Blessing two. Turns out my sloppy husband is incredibly thoughtful, and if he was sucked up into heaven without me, I would be very, very sad.

Blessing three. I am well rested, the kids are out of the house (and again, not somewhere out of my earthly reach), and I can tidy up this mess.

Blessing four. If absence makes the heart grow fonder, this bizarre brush with fake-rapture had me sitting on the couch, counting the many ways I appreciated my exhausting, messy, chaotic, beautiful family.

I sat up and wiped the sleep from my eyes. I checked my phone one more time to see when my husband's message was sent.

Twenty minutes ago? Turns out, he hadn't been gone long.

I grabbed some flip-flops, a cup of coffee, and headed for the door.

After all, my family, my whole heart, was at the park enjoying a beautiful sunny day.

And I didn't want to be left behind.

THE
Badge

OF
Business

THE BADGE OF BUSYNESS

I RAN INTO ONE OF MY FAVORITE PEOPLE THIS WEEK.

We gave birth at the same time, in the same hospital, and in that fresh and terrifying phase of new motherhood, she became one of my closest friends. We texted and met up constantly. Then . . .

I don't know what happened. Maybe just life? Fortunately, we ended up enrolling our daughters in the same toddler ballet class. We were both thrilled. Maybe this would be the new beginning our friendship needed.

As our girls took the floor with their messy buns and precious little tutus, we snapped a few pictures and laughed about how absurdly cute the whole thing was.

"We should really try to get together more often, shouldn't we?" I asked, hoping she was really missing me.

"Yes! Let's do that. Let's plan it right now!"

We looked at the following Monday, which didn't work because her son had soccer.

Then we looked at Tuesday, which didn't work because I had praise band practice at church.

Wednesday was youth group night for her oldest kid, so she spends special time with her youngest at home and uses the down time to catch up on chores.

Thursday was ballet class.

Friday was my son's soccer.

Saturday, Sunday, Monday.

You get the point.

And as the kids finished their thirty minutes of twirling around with bubbles, we hugged, grabbed a selfie, and pledged to do better next week.

In the back of my mind, I knew that next week
wasn't going to be any better.

The whole thing honestly stunk. And it wasn't her fault. This is a phenomenon I've recently noticed in our generation of mothers. We feel a need to justify our motherhood. And we do that by wearing a badge of busyness.

Ask any of your mom friends how they are doing this week, and I bet you a dollar you'll get an answer like this:

"OMG I'm so *tired*. Johnny isn't sleeping, and I volunteered for VBS this week, and I haven't even started slicing the oranges for Addie's soccer game. We have to go here. I have to do this. Ballet is on Thursday! Soccer on Friday! Sunday school is having a picnic, then PTA is Monday!"

If you're like me, you respond with your own rant of similar stresses, because solidarity, right? We are all just mothers living on the verge of insanity!

But I have to wonder . . . why are we doing this? Why *do* we treat exhaustion like it's a badge of honor? Why do we voluntarily pack our calendars to the brim so that the only time we get to actually talk to our children is from the inside of our minivans, traveling from place to place?

Listen to me, Mamas. I get it. This parenting thing is *hard*.

It is exhausting to keep tiny humans fed, clean, and alive. Bonus points if yours are actually happy. Mine whine roughly 51 percent of the time. Really. It's hard to take care of a house, keep the groceries stocked, pets fed, meals cooked, and floors cleaned. At the end of the day, parents are physically pooped. Mentally worn.

It is hard raising kids!

WHY DO WE ALWAYS FEEL THE NEED TO HIT MAXIMUM CAPACITY?

I returned to ballet the following Thursday, somewhat embarrassed that an entire week had passed without so much as a text between my friend and me.

She asked me how I was doing, and I answered exactly how you would expect.

"Ugh, I am so tired." And before I could unload all my "whys," she turned to me and asked, "MK, why do you do this?"

I was taken aback and a little offended. I mean, duh. I'll tell you why.

"I have kids. I am working. I am trying to lose weight. I am volunteering at my church, cutting oranges—you know, I am busy."

And she looked at me dead in the eye and asked me again:

"I mean, *why*? Why are we doing all of this?" She motioned her hands toward the ballet room where our girls were busy chasing bubbles and stomping the hardwood floor with their tap shoes. The teacher switched songs and handed out teddy bears and looked at the clock, praying for the last ten minutes of time to pass quickly.

It was a good question. Mamas . . . why are we doing this?

I don't mean ballet specifically, because let's face it, chubby thighs in pink tights are just delicious. But, why do we say yes to that one more thing that pushes us over the edge? Why do we always feel the need to hit maximum capacity?

Is it because we feel like we aren't enough? Like somehow parenting isn't a taxing enough job for us to stand proud at the end of the day, knowing we raised our kids and did our work. That in itself is incredible.

I'll tell you why I say yes to all these things.

At times, it's because I don't feel like I am enough. At times, it's because I am insecure. I want people to think I am important, and that my voice matters.

So when a writing job pops up at an incredible website, I say yes. And when an agent reaches out to me to write a book, I say yes. And when the church asks me to lead the praise band, I feel affirmed in my talents, so I say yes.

I don't say yes to everything because I have time or because I feel truly inspired. I say yes to things because I believe I need them to prop me up as a person.

And because sometimes, it's scarier to say no.

It's scary to turn something down, even when it's just the school asking you to be class mom.

I know that people say, "Let something go, and if it's meant to be, it'll come back at the right time."

But the thing is, I don't believe that. I believe that sometimes when you say no to things, they don't come back. You simply have to make peace with that.

But you know what the truth is, Mamas? Your yeses are not what define you. They don't prop you up.

These "busyness badges" will never make you important.

Because you already *are* important.

You are created in God's image. You are beautiful. You are a parent to an incredible tiny human who relies on you to teach them the ways of the world.

That's a huge freaking job.

And no matter what anyone tells you, it's a big enough job to fill up all day, every day.

So should we continue to do things that inspire us? Absolutely. But we shouldn't say yes to every single thing that comes along. Because in the end, it's not what we say yes to that will define us.

It's what we say NO to.

The most powerful thing in the world you can do as a mother, as a person, is look at your life and determine what your no needs to be.

Is it that second job? Is it volunteering? Maybe it's just your kid's karate class.

Say no. Practice it with me: NO.

And when you learn to say no to the things you don't need, that will liberate you to say all the right yeses.

Yes to spending time with your babies. Yes to mental health and physical rest. Yes to growing spiritually.

Mamas, we are going to be exhausted. It's just that season in life. And there will come a time when this season will pass and we will look back on it, realizing just how beautiful it all was.

But we won't look back and think: Wow, I am so glad I was busy. I am so glad I added that extra swim lesson to our schedule. I am so glad I sliced one thousand oranges for the Little Ninjas soccer squad.

Look at your life today and ask: What do I need to say no to? What is my best no?

Then make no your new word. Make no your friend.

Because when you say no, you will find that your life has margin.

You know those lined pieces of paper that we used back when we walked to school uphill both ways? (Do people use those anymore?) Well, there's a reason the paper has margins, and it's the same reason your life should have margins. It gives you room for mistakes. Room to breathe. A little extra space when a sentence, or an activity, runs late.

Make saying no a thing. Give your life some margin.

Today I'm looking at my life, and I'm going to make some changes. I need room to breathe. I need room for error.

And I need to learn that I am good enough, important enough, and I matter enough exactly as I am. No add-ons.

And you are too, Mama.

You are, too.

WHEN YOU SAY NO, YOU WILL FIND THAT YOUR LIFE HAS MARGIN.

ACKNOWLEDGMENTS

I have to start by thanking Mama, who stood by the bedside of my dead pet cricket when I was in fifth grade, keeping a straight face and wearing all black. You understood my need for melodrama and nurtured every manifestation of my weirdo genetics. And to my Joe Joe, who rubbed my feet as I wrote three chapters on my iPhone over July 4th weekend. I love you.

Thanks to my Daddy. You sharpen and challenge me, and remain a soft landing place whenever I've screwed up big. I always feel safe calling you no matter what crazy thing I've done. I love you. And thanks to DD, for holding down our Huntsville home and loving me as your very own. I need to confess that I hid a few five-hundred-dollar bills under the Monopoly board that fateful night. Will you forgive me?

Thanks to Kurt and Suzi, for fully accepting the crazy woman your son chose to marry. You have supported every dream I've ever had and never once made me feel silly when my dreams changed (which was often). I am lucky to have you. And Ben . . . I love you so freaking much. But I'll never let you live down the days of being "Tron."

Thanks to my sister, Karen Leigh, for always demanding more of me than I wanted to ask of myself. You are my hero.

Thanks to my brother, Ty, for the childhood adventures we have shared. The magic of those memories is drenched in these pages. I hope you can find a little glimmer of the past and smile.

To my baby brother, Jackson, for reminding me that powerful faith can come in tiny packages. You taught me a lot about being a mom, and I'm so proud of who you have become.

And my brother, Justin (and Beth!), for the immense grace you exemplify. You are an inspiration, and I love you. You'll be an amazing dad.

To my husband, Ian. You believed in me, B. From now until the day the waves wash us both away, you are my person. I love spending time with you.

Thanks to my children, Ben and Holland, for filling my life (and these pages) with laughter and joy. You are the best thing I've ever done.

Thank you to Mrs. Ruth Messick Hooks. You taught me to love language and empowered me with beautiful words. Your classroom and your ability to teach were magic. Thank you.

Thank you, Lauren Arieux Bryan, for using your professional position to give me this life-changing opportunity. I owe you forever.

Thank you, Karen Longino, for believing in me as a writer and a person. Your work makes dreams come true. Pretty sure that makes you a fairy godmother.

Thank you, Natalie Hanemann, my editor. You had so much more than stray words to deal with. At times you had a stray writer. You handled both with grace.

Thank you, Michele Richter, my 007, who had to Jerry Maguire me on multiple occasions. Next round in NYC is on me. Send more cat pictures.

Thank you, Sara and Meredith, for walking through life with me. We are the three best friends anyone could have, and I miss you right now. Even though we probably just talked two minutes ago.

Thanks to my Nanna for loving me like your own and allowing my drunk bird to live in your garage. You've always believed in me.

Thank you, Meredith Masony, for being a giver. It's who you are, and you don't think anything of it, but somebody should tell you: you are amazing. Thank you for your support. It is invaluable, and I'll never forget it.

Thank you to my dear, dear Alex White. For taking me under your wing and convincing me that, yes, I am a real writer who belongs "out there."

Thanks to Cristofs and Waffle House in Fort Myers, Florida. The coffee and office space were much appreciated. Special thanks to Ms. Cynthia, Betty, Shannon, and Christian.

Thanks to my New Hope family, especially Mrs. Pam, for supporting my family's faith journey.

Thanks to Joann, the boss mama at TJP. You have loved us so dang well.

Thank you to Coco for being my friend and sister. For loving my babies and keeping my life in order. I thank God every day for our friendship. And to Hannah and Steven . . . my extended family. Thanks for caring for my babies while I worked on this dream.

Thank you, Jill Smokler. For paving a way for me and thousands of other writers. For publishing my words first and for accepting me into your fold. I admire you so much.

Thank you to the Drakes. My dear friends and original beta readers. Sorry I never finished "In Alpin Wood." Hope you love this book. And our other Incredible, Clarebear. I miss you so.

Thank you, Goldners, for sending a family member to my rescue any time I was in crisis. Eliot, for hashing out essays over lunch. Melissa, for never holding back an honest opinion. Thanks for adopting the Backstroms and loving us well.

Thank you, Chels, for being my person. Pink ladies forever.

Thank you, Lauren, for thirty years of friendship. You are always loyal, and I don't deserve you.

Thank you, Lindsey, for guiding me through my tumultuous college years. I'm so glad you finally got your Saint Bernards.

Thank you to #WriteOrDie, especially Lauri and Kimberly. We've really seen one another grow, haven't we? I love you so.

To Lindsay, my Songbird and dearest friend, and Heather, the OG mama in pajamas.

Thanks to Carli Karluk and the WDW Wolfpack for loving me well, supporting my voice, and introducing me to The Mighty Acorn Foundation.

Thanks to every Mom Babble follower (I see you, Joy!) and supporter I've had these past five years. I wouldn't be a writer without y'all.

A special thanks to the Drakes (again), the Housholders, and Bae Hart (of the Bae Hive Photography). I'm so grateful your beautiful photos filled these pages. Your family memories captured my heart and made this vision come to life.

Thank you, Mike Salisbury and Yates and Yates for believing in me and taking me on as a new voice.

breathe almost done . . .

Thank you, God. It feels silly saying this on paper, because really, what a small offering to bring before the throne. But here is my talent, Father. I did my best, and I hope I make you proud.

Words will never be enough, but that's the currency I'm dealing with these days. So once more, from the bottom of my heart, to everyone who has been a part of this journey . . .

Thank you.

ABOUT THE AUTHOR

MARY KATHERINE (MK) BACKSTROM is a viral blogger and the founder of Mom Babble, an online community of 250,000 followers. Her video content boasts more than 30 million views, and she is the 2017 recipient of *The Today Show* Iris Award for best parenting writer. Mary Katherine's work has been featured on the *Today* Show, *Washington Post*, *Good Morning America*, *Ellen*, and more.